The
BOOK
OF BOOKS

TONY JEARY

THE RESULTS GUY™

The
BOOK
OF BOOKS

THE BEST
OF HIS
FIRST 50 TITLES

The Book of Books

©2018 by Tony Jeary

Published by Results Faster! Publishing

Published in association with Larry Carpenter of Clovercroft Publishing

Cover design by Debbie Manning Sheppard

Interior Design by Adept Content Solutions

ISBN: 978-1-945507-96-0

Printed in the United States of America

CONTENTS

FOREWORD

For most books, someone who knows the author writes the foreword to validate and endorse the contents of the book. This is a unique book, and unique books deserve a unique foreword.

This *Book of Books* is literally a collection of the highlights of the best takeaways of the first fifty books I've authored; we thought it would be fitting, then, for the foreword of this book to be a collection of extracted highlights from the forewords, endorsements, and introductions written specifically for my best books.

"Whether we like it or not, people who articulate well, both privately and in front of a group, are generally perceived to be more intelligent and possess greater leadership qualities.
There's no doubt about it: being able to speak effectively is vitally important, whether the intent is to ask for a raise or persuade an individual or company to take a specific action. . . . Tony Jeary is a master at handling these occasions, and more importantly, he has developed a system that is easy to learn, understand, and implement, so your own effectiveness will quickly improve.
It's good stuff!"

—Zig Ziglar, Book 1: *Inspire Any Audience (1997)*

"Within these pages you will learn how to get the very most out of yourself, both as an individual and in your relationships with others. You will learn how to set better goals, make better plans, and develop better strategies for achieving those goals—on schedule. Tony Jeary is one of the most insightful and intelligent writers, thinkers, speakers, and presenters in America today. . . . Get ready for an exciting ride!"

—Brian Tracy, Book 10: *Success Acceleration* (2002)

"My good friend Tony Jeary and I have worked together on several projects over the years. We produced a video series together called "Inspire Any Audience." I soon learned that Tony has a gift for helping people articulate things they want to communicate but simply do not know how. I found Tony to be extremely knowledgeable in the area of communication— the field of study to which I have devoted my entire life. Even though Tony knows an incredible amount of information and is an accomplished professional speaker, I have seen him show gentleness and be helpful to many who aspire to be better speakers."

—Zig Ziglar, Book 14: *Presenting with Style* (2006)

"What Tony shares in *Strategic Acceleration* about clarity, focus, and execution is extremely valuable for anyone wanting to excel."

—*SUCCESS* Magazine, Book 37: *Strategic Acceleration* (2009)

"We decided that I would conduct lengthy, personal interviews with thirty of Tony's best long-term customers. What I discovered in those interviews was amazing to me... [It] also convinced me to finally join with Tony on a full-time basis and become the president of his company. . . . What did we discover in the interviews of our customers? The interviews kept producing the same three words over and over again: Clarity—Focus—Execution! Tony was helping people get clarity for their strategic vision, helping them focus on the things that really matter, and helping them develop powerful strategies to execute their vison. As a result, his customers were able to improve their results significantly, within time frames that they had not believed possible."

—Jim Norman, Book 37: *Strategic Acceleration* (2009)

"In the game of life, what we don't know can blindside us. *Ultimate Health* is about creating awareness and guiding us along the most positive preventive medicine path."

—Troy Aikman, Super Bowl MVP, Book 35: *Ultimate Health* (2013)

"I can tell you that I've never seen a person be more diligent and persistent about executing a strategic plan. . . . As I have watched Tony build a company with a client list made up with some of the smartest business people in the world, I've spent a lot of time contemplating just what it is about Tony that separates him from other strategic consultants. Here's the answer: Tony Jeary helps people think differently! He does it by the example he models, by the practices he teaches, and by the open way he shares his personal and professional life with others. This book, *Living in the Black,* is a classic example of Tony's open approach to sharing information. It comes out of a sincere and honest desire to help others become the absolute best they can be while inspiring them to experience life at its fullest."

—Jim Norman, Book 42: *Living in the Black* (2014)

"You're never too young or too old to benefit from great advice from others—or to give it away—and you can never reach a level of success where you no longer need it... [Tony] and Jay have a mutual friend, Peter Thomas, who has been a serial entrepreneur for more than four decades, specializing in franchising and real estate. Peter has developed billions of dollars in real estate projects, including shopping centers, apartments, condominiums, and golf courses, and he built Century 21 all across Canada. The second time Tony met him, Peter arranged for them to meet on his yacht. With all of his successes, within one hour of that meeting, he said to Tony, "I want you to be my coach for life." . . . Jay has been Tony's business mentor for years. Yet, because he believes so strongly in the impact that great advice can have, he recently took the management team of a company he founded to Tony's studio for a strategic planning session and asked Tony to "pour it on!" The results have been no less than amazing. In the past 90 days, the company has enjoyed more profit growth than they experienced in the prior twelve months. More importantly, they have now focused on a niche market that they are uniquely qualified to serve."

—Jay Rodgers, Book 45: *Advice Matters* (2015)

"I am very thankful for my dad, Tony Jeary, who helped guide me in decisions and direction in my life. He did a great job at pouring a great amount of knowledge into my life. He is very knowledgeable and always there to answer a question. . . . One of my favorite things that he did was show me the world... I think it is very important to see the world from others' perspective, and traveling was a great way to do that. . . . Connections were a theme that my dad taught me. A quote my dad said that stuck with me is, 'It's not about the grades you make, but the number of hands you shake.' I have learned the power of personal connections."

—Paige Jeary (Age 20), Book 49: *Family Wealth* (2017)

INTRODUCTION

As a strategist to high-achieving leaders around the globe, my life's work is impacting the thinking and the results of some of the brightest people in the world. One of my biggest blessings is personally coaching the presidents of Fortune 500 companies like Walmart, Sam's Club, Ford, Samsung, American Airlines, Firestone, New York Life, and many others. Inspiring them and their teams, in both their professional and personal lives, is my passion.

Some describe me as an encourager who helps people expand their thinking to win more. As I've traveled through life, I've observed many best practices, uncovered many *Blind Spots*, and had many "ah-ha" moments that have all changed my thinking. Each epiphany—whether it came through an experience of my own or from someone else's wisdom—has led me to strategically and intentionally live out the distinctions I learned through that experience. Over time, after seeing substantial results by living them out and proving them in my own life, I began teaching the distinctions to my clients. And the result was often a book, which allowed me the privilege of touching and changing the thinking of even more people with the life and business lessons I'd learned.

Author's NOTE

I began my professional career helping people to develop and deliver presentations that would achieve their desired goal. Over the years of research I have developed many tools and strategic methodologies for doing this. If I were to rewrite these books today, they would include my additional thinking and perspectives, so I have included areas of "Expanded Thinking" that update you on my current thinking and best practices related to certain books and subjects.

Many of the "presentation" books are variations on a theme. My purpose was to apply learnings and methodologies to different situations. A one-on-one presentation is not the same as a seminar to fifty people or a speech to 5,000. Pitching a product is not the same as pitching an idea. Distinctions that apply to team leaders who are informing and motivating their teams will be different than those for CEOs who are presenting their vision to their employees, which may not even be done before a live audience. So many of these books necessarily cover much of the same ground but are applied to different situations.

In 2007 I began a new chapter in my life with the book *Strategic Acceleration*. This book presented a methodology for transforming lives and organizations. *Strategic Acceleration* took me from the art

I've authored fifty books (to date) that have all served to complement and enhance my practice of enriching people's lives. The book you hold in your hands is a collection of the very best life-changing content from those fifty books—an anthology of the first two-plus decades of my life's work of helping others win.

My hope for you as you read this book is that you will learn from my experiences: the ups and downs, and the highs and the lows. After personally testing and applying the principles, methodologies, and best practices you're about to read, I can respectfully say that my life is better than I ever thought possible. I am supremely blessed and grateful that I get to do what I love every day, which is helping others and science of presentations to the art and science of strategic transformation. However, as with presentations, the methodologies for strategic transformation are applied differently in different situations and contexts. As a result, please note that there is some intentional redundancy of content for different applications.

Finally, throughout my life I have been fascinated with the idea that business success does not always lead to personal happiness—or at least total happiness. The result has been a lifelong study on how one can lead to the other. You will find several books that deal with achieving happiness through applying my mantra of thinking strategically in all areas of life to family, personal health, and wealth management. These books are based on both my personal experiences and the experiences of others I know well who have achieved that elusive balance that brings true happiness.

I hope you find practical lessons and inspiration in the book capsules provided here. If you see a particular book you would like a copy of, visit Amazon, iTunes, or any of the myriad other websites that carry my books. If you prefer, you can purchase a book from our website at tonyjeary.com, and we'll be happy to send an autographed copy to you.

achieve extraordinary results.

This book is also a testament to the impact that people and experiences have had on *my* life. In the *Book of Books* I share some of the connections and moments that have changed my life forever, and, if you've been exposed to any of my teachings, possibly even yours.

Those layers of impact have all come together to form and reinforce a recurring two-pronged theme:

1. Change your thinking to be intentionally strategic about everything you do.

2. Look for ways to consistently give more value than people expect.

I propose that if you do those two things, you can have results beyond your wildest dreams in every facet of your life. That's the theme I live by, and the results have indeed proved phenomenal. That's also the theme I've invested my life teaching to others.

I would venture to say that you have probably experienced one or more life-changing events in your life. Am I right? Most people have. One of mine (which I'll share more about in the book) was something very special that happened when I was just sixteen years old. That's when I was first introduced to personal development and the awesome power of learning by example, when I was given the book *How to Win Friends and Influence People* by Dale Carnegie. This book affected the whole course of my life and led me to believe in the life-affirming and life-altering power of the written word.

Someone once shared this powerful one-liner with me: Books can go where you can't go and stay longer than you can stay. I knew, then, that well-written books were the best way to give more people the benefit of what I had learned and to spread the concepts that have helped me and so many others achieve extraordinary results.

Since each book featured here was written as a result of a specific epiphany or inspiration, each one truly has a story behind it. As you read, I think you'll discover interesting links among many of the books. Taken all together, the stories paint a picture of the impact people and events have had on my life and the value I've been able to pass along as a result. I've dedicated my life to giving high value to others by helping them achieve extraordinary results, and that's the same value I promise to deliver to you in this book.

This morning, my American Airlines app showed that I have travelled 4.7 million miles with them to date. (American Airlines is one of our biggest and most long-standing clients.) I have personally worked in over fifty countries with thousands of clients, and I've developed over three hundred training courses. I also author a monthly column for *SUCCESS* magazine called "Ask The RESULTS Guy™," I've hosted a TV show called *Success Acceleration,* and I've been on the front cover of many business magazines across the globe. My agency, Tony Jeary International, has advised some two dozen families from the Forbes 400 Richest People in America list. We touch millions of lives around the world every year.

That's my life professionally. Personally, I've been rich, broke, sued, overweight, embezzled, and divorced, and I've endured such extreme lows that it's hard to believe I'm standing where I am today. Instead of focusing on the negative and calling it quits, I put my energy and mind where it counts most. I focused on the positives in life—God, family, clients, customers, and business colleagues whom I also have the privilege of calling my friends. I'm blessed to have been married for almost three decades and to have two highly successful adult daughters and, so far, one passionate, gifted son-in-law. I currently live and work on my estate (so my office is steps away from home) and bring the world's best into my RESULTS Studio where I advise them and we share and strategize together. (At the time of this writing we're beginning construction on a world-class RESULTS Center that I'm building with my long-time friend and partner Jack Furst.) I continually look for ways (like with this new specially designed building) to give over-the-top value every day by helping our clients accomplish extraordinary results, faster, and turn their visions into reality. I'm sharing this with you *not to boast, but to show you that I live what I teach and practice what I preach.*

I would be remiss without mentioning here two people who have probably had the most profound influence on my life and my results— my father and Jim Norman. My father is the person who taught me the mantra, "Give value; do more than is expected." I've carried out that mantra in everything I've done, and the results speak for themselves.

Jim Norman served as my coach and president for twenty years before he passed away a couple of years ago. He's the person who helped me realize that my strong point was helping people think more effectively. That's when I adopted the moniker The RESULTS Guy™, and my focus since that time has become helping smart, aggressive, successful people think better, document it, and then execute strategically.

As a result of Jim's influence, my life as The RESULTS Guy™ is not just about making more money—it's about making *life better*. If you're thinking right, you can be intentionally strategic about everything you do, and that leads to incredible results. Many high achievers are strong in the business area of their lives, and yet they have issues in other areas. They may be in bad health, or their marriage or family may be less than they desire. They're often committed to getting better results in their business; however, they fail to implement strategic thinking and focus in the other areas of life where they need to improve. Over the years, I've been able to help many people see that they're falling short in a certain area of life because that powerful piece is missing—they're not thinking strategically in that area.

Jim Norman had the capacity to think on a higher plane strategically than virtually anyone I've ever known. He was the president of Zig Ziglar's company for six years (he was also Zig's son-in-law), and it took me ten years after he left Zig's company to persuade him to become my president. He agreed to be my coach during those years and then finally became my president in 2006. Over the next ten years he guided my thinking and directly impacted my results before he passed away in 2016. I can easily say that Jim Norman changed my thinking, and therefore my life, as much or more than any other person. I can attribute much of my phenomenal results (and maybe yours, too) to his brilliant mind and mentorship.

As you go through this book, you'll catch the overall theme of strategically thinking to improve your results. When Jim passed away, we were in the process of writing a profound book together about that very subject ... thinking! I want to honor him and his legacy by wrapping up this *Book of Books* with a chapter from *Thinking: Change Your Thinking, Change Your Results*, which actually serves to tie together all of the great insights from my fifty books.

My team and I were very strategic in putting this *Book of Books* together. We wanted to give you what has stood out over time as the best of the best. The principles we've included in this book have impacted my results and the results of thousands of other people. I'm confident you'll be motivated by the insightful stories that have impacted so many others.

I'm also excited to introduce another tool we've created to help you get the most from this book. The "If You Want to Know" section follows the introduction, and it shows you where to find information on any of twenty-eight topics you may want to know more about. Let's say you want to know more about "clarity," for example. You can find "clarity" on the left side of the matrix, and it will tell you which of the fifty books cover that topic. Then you can look at the Contents page and go directly to the book(s) that will give you that information.

My hope is that this special book will forever impact your life, just as so many people have impacted mine. Dig in.

Serving the best,
Tony

If You Want to Know	
# Concept	Books Hitting these Concepts
Belief Window	Success Acceleration, Strategic Acceleration
Brand	RESULTS Faster!, Strategic Acceleration, Presenting with Style, Rich Relationships, Living Life Smiling
Clarity	Strategic Acceleration, Designing Your Own Life, Advice Matters, Strategic Parenting, Living in the Black, Leverage, Conclusion
Coaching	One-to-One Presentations, Life is a Series of Presentations, Leadership 25, Business Ground Rules, Strategic Parenting, Advice Matters
Collaboration	Happy Families, Training Other People to Train, RESULTS Faster!
Culture	Strategic Acceleration, Strategies for Business Peak Performance, Life is a Series of Presentations, Business Ground Rules, Leverage, Strategic Selling
Delegation	How to Gain 100 Extra Minutes a Day, Thinking Pays!, Conclusion
Effective Meetings	Meeting Magic, We've Got to Stop Meeting Like This, We've Got to Start Meeting and Emailing Like This
Efficiency	Leverage, RESULTS Faster!, How to Gain 100 Extra Minutes a Day
Execution	Strategic Acceleration, Success Acceleration, RESULTS Faster!
Focus	Leadership 25, Leverage, Strategic Acceleration, RESULTS Faster!
Force Multipliers	RESULTS Faster!
Goal Setting	Designing Your Own Life, RESULTS Faster!
Happy	Strategic Parenting, Happy Families, Fun Things to do as Kids, Living Life Smiling
High Leverage Activities	Leverage, Strategic Acceleration, RESULTS Faster!
Mentorship	Advice Matters, Strategic Parenting, Living in the Black

(Continued)

If You Want to Know *(Continued)*	
# Concept	Books Hitting these Concepts
Personal Improvement	Life is a Series of Presentations, Success Acceleration, RESULTS Faster!, Communication Mastery: NLP Made Simple, Neurolinguistic Communication P.A., Business Ground Rules
Persuasion	Persuade Any Audience, Communication Mastery: NLP Made Simple, Neurolinguistic Communication P.A.
Presentations	Inspire Any Audience, A Collection of Ice Breakers, Attention Keepers and Activities, Speaking Spice, Persuade Any Audience, Presenting with Style, Winning Seminars, 136 Effective Presentation Tips, The Complete Guide to Effective Facilitation, One-to-One Presentations, Speaking from the Top, Nervous to Natural, Presentation Mastery for Realtors, Purpose-Filled Presentations
Prioritization	Leverage, RESULTS Faster!, How to Gain 100 Extra Minutes a Day
Production Before Perfection (PBP)	Success Acceleration
Significance	Purpose-Filled Presentations, Living Life Smiling
Speed	Strategic Acceleration
Team Building/ Synergy	Change—Mindset Matters
Thinking	Thinking Pays!, Conclusion
Time Effectiveness	How to Gain 100 Extra Minutes a Day
Values	Designing Your Own Life, RESULTS Faster!
Visualization	Designing Your Own Life, RESULTS Faster!

BOOK 1
INSPIRE ANY AUDIENCE
PROVEN SECRETS OF THE PROS
FOR POWERFUL PRESENTATIONS

My mentor and good friend, the late Zig Ziglar, described this book as "the ultimate presenter's handbook." Whether you're presenting to five people, five hundred, or five thousand, *Inspire Any Audience* delivers everything you need to become a polished, professional, and inspiring presenter. In fact, this book has been compared to a comprehensive course in public speaking, as it provides distinctions that enable you to effectively present to anyone, anywhere, with confidence. The truth is, *when you present like a pro, you get results.*

My first attempt at inspiring an audience thirty years ago didn't turn out so well. I was in Seattle, Washington, starting out on my first forty-city speaking tour. In spite of all my preparation, I was so nervous that I didn't realize until after I'd been speaking for thirty minutes that half of my overhead slides were upside down!

Thankfully, I doubled down on studying and learning all I could about presentations after that experience. Eventually Chrysler hired me to train their leadership and managers and then all of their trainers. I ended up building a large international training organization, and in the nineties I trained people on three continents in more than thirty countries. Through the years I developed a unique and effective methodology—called Presentation Mastery™—that takes a strategic approach to presentation effectiveness, versus just teaching presentation as a skill.

As I was training other people to train, I realized there was a huge need to put into a book many of the distinctions that had eventually made me successful at doing that over the years, and to take it beyond just training and make it about positively *inspiring* any audience. Good presenters hold an audience's attention; exceptional speakers inspire their audience to take action and get results!

What does the book say?

The book lays out the seven solid foundational ideas that form the cornerstone for inspiring any audience as well as the many techniques I learned over the years that will help you polish your presentation effectiveness and improve your ability to inspire any audience. Any time you present, you want to inspire your audience to do something—perhaps it's to think differently or to take an action, or maybe it's to buy into something. The book is a valuable reference guide that is chock-full of tips, powerful quotes, checklists, matrices, assessments, evaluations, and other tools that will help you do just that.

How will the book help you?

By studying and gaining an indelible understanding of the Seven Foundational Secrets® listed below, you will have a greater impact every time you present, because you'll be better able to inspire any audience to take whatever action you want them to take. And by making the 3-D Outline™ an essential tool you use each time you prepare for a presentation, you'll be able to see the big picture and sort through the material you need to produce for your presentation right away, as it helps you determine not only *what* you want to say, but also *why* and *how* to say it (hence the name 3-D, or 3-Dimensional). We've included a 3-D Outline™ template below the Seven Foundational Secrets® listed below.

The Seven Foundational Secrets®

Foundational Secret No. 1: Funneling Process. This is a surveying tool. Its intent is to uncover your audience's hidden needs and wants, thus guaranteeing that your presentation is on target. This process takes all the things you could do—those hundreds of possibilities— and funnels them down to a solid core of doable, reachable objectives. By taking these few simple steps, you should be able to more clearly define your objectives, and hence your message.

Foundational Secret No. 2: Four Subconscious Tensions. Understanding how to relieve the four subconscious tensions common to all audiences will increase audience acceptance. Tension exists between:

1. Audience members and other audience members. If people don't know the person they are sitting next to or haven't seen them for a while, there is often a temptation to talk to them, or they could simply want to find out what's up with their

audience neighbor. Using a great icebreaker to get people to connect with the audience members around them at the beginning of a presentation can relieve that tension and shift their attention to your agenda instead of their own.

2. Audience members and the presenter. Audience members often ask themselves whether they are eager to hear your presentation. They want to know what's in it for them. Give value right up front by letting them know you're organized, you're prepared, and you have something valuable they want to hear.

3. Audience members and the materials the presenter provides for them. If you distribute all of your handouts at the beginning of your presentation, participants are often distracted because they're looking through the handouts instead of listening to you. To diffuse this tension, you may want to layer your handouts to distribute just as you are beginning to cover that particular material.

4. Audience members and their environment. You're both the host and the manager of your experience, so before your presentation starts, make sure the seating and temperature are comfortable and that there are no barriers between the audience and you or the screen. Also do anything else you can to make the environment conducive for your audience to focus only on you and your message. Eliminate all environmental distractions—including (but not limited to) lighting, weak sound, spacing, and overcrowded seating. Control and manage everything you can.

Foundational Secret No. 3: Trust Transference. Without trust, there is no buy-in. You can use *Trust Transference* to ignite buy-in every time you're in front of the room. Use a book, an authority figure, a quote from a famous person, or research documents, for example, to transfer trust from a well-known and respected source to your own message and to convince your audience to take the action you're asking them to take. By knowing your audience—what they like and who and what they trust—you can strategically speed the rapport process and bond more quickly and easily. And finally, when you're at the top of your game you can use what I've termed as *Peer Trust Transference*—smartly utilizing a respected audience member to validate you thinking, request, or teaching point.

Foundational Secret No. 4: Business Entertainment™. This is a must. If your audience isn't captivated, you can't be assured of their full attention, and without their attention, you can't be effective. There are many forms of *Business Entertainment™*. For now, though, let's just call it the appropriate "fun factor." People like to have fun. Right? The fact is, most people don't tell good jokes; however, there are many other ways to bring great entertainment value and humor to your presentations, like using interesting facts, fun props, games, skits, music, role-playing, quizzes, trivia, and of course showing funny videos. I personally like to give away crisp, new one-dollar bills to facilitate humor and bring involvement. Look for ways to not be boring and bring in the appropriate *Business Entertainment*.

Foundational Secret No. 5: Verbal Surveying. This a powerful technique you can use to get feedback during your entire presentation—whether it's a fifteen-minute speech, a three-day training seminar, or a two-hour sales presentation. Simply by asking your audience, you can know more how to pace your delivery and whether or not you are covering your subject in the right amount of detail. During your presentation, simply ask your audience: "Are you getting what I'm saying?" "Am I going too fast?" "Would you like me to cover this in more detail?" Ask, get their input, and then adjust your presentation as you move through the material to ensure you stay on target with the way they want to receive your message. Remember, if you want to be a master presenter, make it about helping your audience members win.

Foundational Secret No. 6: Targeted Polling. A great way to decrease nervousness and relate to your audience, as well as to get insights about them and establish advocates, is to take advantage of opportunities to talk one-on-one with audience members. (Plan a time to do this just a few minutes before you start your talk, as people show up early, or perhaps just as importantly, during a break or lunch.) Ask what they really want, what's important to them, or what their expectations might be. Request suggestions. Then adjust your presentation accordingly and be right on target as you begin or continue with your presentation. Remember, when possible, it's important to give your audience what they want. People like to be given individual attention, so make every opportunity work for you. *Foundational Secret No. 7: Audience Closure.* Proper closure proves you have met and exceeded your audience's expectations. As you transition between points *and* as you end your presentation, summarize and reinforce to your audience both the value they received and the actions you want them to take. Executed properly, closure ensures that audience members leave your presentation as owners of you message and as ambassadors for you and your subject matter.

The 3-D Outline™

Presentation Title		Delivery Date	
Audience		Start Time	
Objectives		End Time	
Final Preparation Checklist					
#	Time	What	Why	How	Who
1.					
2.					
3.					
4.					
5.					
Total Time					

In short, *Inspire Any Audience* delivers the confidence and professionalism you need to succeed in front of your audience—any audience!

BOOK 2
STRATEGIES FOR BUSINESS PEAK PERFORMANCE

Strategies for Business Peak Performance delivers exactly what the name implies—practical, proven techniques and strategies that will help both entrepreneurs and managers improve their businesses to ensure maximum results.

Years ago, one of my clients called me and said, "I have a friend you need to hire as your business manager." He knew I had been looking for the right person for that position. I trusted his judgment, so I said, "Great! I'd like to meet him." He connected me with Dan Miller, who turned out to be an exceptional fit. In fact, he was phenomenal because he understood financial and business matters better than most people I knew.

One of the first things Dan did was assess where we were as a company. Interestingly, I have Dan to thank for helping me identify a *Blind Spot* I didn't even know I had all those years ago—not understanding the enormous value of strategically assessing and evaluating your business (with measurements) to discover the gap between where you are and where you want to go. Together, we began to recognize an obvious need for helping other business owners and managers assess their strengths and weaknesses and implement strategic management practices in five major areas—Finance, Operations, Marketing/Sales, Employee Management, and Quality Assurance—to help them get more of the results they're looking for. So, we carefully crafted the book *Strategies for Business Peak Performance* to fill that need.

What does the book say?

We start the book with a preliminary analysis so you can easily assess your strengths and weaknesses in the five major areas of Finance, Operations, Marketing/Sales, Employee Management, and Quality Assurance. Then we share strategies and techniques in the rest of the book that will help you become a consultant to your own business as you apply our best practices to the specific areas within your organization.

How will the book help you?

The Preliminary Analysis is a fact-finding process designed to obtain data that will help determine what problems, if any, exist in a given business. Since it has proven to be one of the main takeaways from the book, we have included it here. We recommend that you utilize this assessment yourself to see if it opens your eyes to a few *Blind Spots* as well. Are there any areas where you need to change your thinking and be more strategic to get better results?

Directions: Carefully consider the issues listed in the first column and determine where your business is in each area. Then check the appropriate box between one and ten, with ten being the strongest, to indicate whether the business is doing well in that area of if there is room for improvement.

#	Audit Point	Needs Improvement							Strong		
		1	2	3	4	5	6	7	8	9	10
Financial Area											
1a	Objectives clear for all employees										
1b	Objectives clear for management										
2a	Written business plan implemented										
2b	Is the current entity effective?										
3a	How is your banking relationship?										
3b	How are your borrowing and cash flow?										
4a	Profitability this quarter										
4b	Profitability this year										
4c	Profitability previous year										
4d	Overall profitability										
4e	Future profitability										
5a	Accuracy of forecasting										
Operations											
6a	Company organizational structure										
6b	Organizational structure understood										
6c	Organizational charts										
7a	Company mission statement clear										

(Continued)

#	Audit Point	Needs Improvement							Strong		
		1	2	3	4	5	6	7	8	9	10
8a	Company time management principles										
8b	Company use of delegation systems										
9a	Telephone equipment										
9b	Company telephone etiquette										
9c	Company communication										
10a	Company use of consultants										
11a	Company policy and procedures										
11b	Company policy and procedures										
11c	Understanding of policy and procedure										
12a	Information flow										
12b	Company use of charts and graphs										
12c	Company forms										
13a	Company values										
13b	Company mission										
13c	Company vision defined										
Marketing/Sales											
14a	Marketing audit										
15a	External presentations										
15b	Internal presentations										
16a	Compensation in line with objectives										

(Continued)

#	Audit Point	Needs Improvement							Strong		
		1	2	3	4	5	6	7	8	9	10
17a	Company sales results										
17b	Company sales tools										
17c	Sales training										
18a	Market share										
18b	Understanding market share										
19a	Advertising programs										
19b	Advertising competitiveness										
19c	Advertising results										
19d	Branding identity										
20a	Telephone for P.R.										
20b	Company follow-up										
Employee Management											
21a	Staff evaluation systems										
22a	Job descriptions (HLAs)										
22b	Formulating job descriptions										
23a	Recruiting systems										
23b	Hiring systems										
24a	Employee appraisal and evaluation										
25a	Staff/employee longevity										
26a	Termination procedures										
Quality Assurance											
27a	Customer satisfaction										
28a	Teamwork										
28b	Employee attitudes										

(Continued)

#	Audit Point	Needs Improvement							Strong		
		1	2	3	4	5	6	7	8	9	10
29a	Effective meetings										
30a	Training										
31a	Effective written communication										
32a	Computer hardware										
32b	Computer software										
33a	Using outside consultants										
33b	Miscellaneous forms										

Quality assurance demands metrics that measure quality.

If you find you have challenges and would like to consider our help in any of these areas, we invite you to reach out to us to discuss your situation. Contact us at info@tonyjeary.com to see how we can help you with the many best practices and the arsenal of tools I've pulled together over the years.

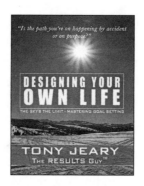

"Is the path you're on happening by accident or on purpose?"

DESIGNING YOUR
OWN LIFE
THE SKY'S THE LIMIT · MASTERING GOAL SETTING

TONY JEARY
THE RESULTS GUY™

BOOK 3
DESIGNING YOUR OWN LIFE

What would your life look like if you could personally design it the way you want it?

Designing Your Own Life is a powerful application workbook that helps you do just that. It guides you through the process of identifying your deepest values and aspirations, clarifying your purpose, identifying your life's mission, and strategically setting goals to help you achieve a life designed to your own personal specifications.

As I mentioned, in 1977, when I was just sixteen years old, I had my initial exposure to personal development when Jinx Thompson, my girlfriend's dad, gave me Dale Carnegie's book *How to Win Friends and Influence People*. Little did I know at the time that reading that book would ultimately lead me to living out my own life's mission of helping people grow and create more of the results they want.

Reading the book also made me realize that books have the power to change people's lives—that's why I author so many. After it opened my eyes to the world of personal development, one of the first experts I came across in that field was Zig Ziglar. I was fascinated with Zig and his teachings on goal-setting, so I personally started studying and setting goals. That began my journey of studying the best, setting more goals than any person I've ever met, proving out that goal-setting really does work, and then teaching those concepts to high-achievers (like you) all over the world.

My quest eventually led me to one of the best goal-setters in the world, Paul J. Meyer, the founder of Success Motivation Institute (SMI). After I went broke in 1986 (see my story below), I went out and bought virtually every audio cassette SMI had, and I listened to those audios over and over again. One of the audios planted a powerful, life-impacting seed in my mind that ultimately defined my future. It claimed that if a person would study a subject for thirty minutes a day for one year, they would become an expert on that subject. I thought, *What if I studied success and results an hour a day for the rest of my life? Then no one would be able to touch me in terms of the value I could provide.* So that's what I've done. I set out to find the best concepts on success and goal-setting and studied them until I became the leading expert on the subject in the world. In other words, I was intentionally strategic about studying everything I could find so I could mold my thinking and become an expert on helping others get results.

My search led me to my good friend and mentor Brian Tracy. I was infatuated by Brian's teachings and in awe of his discipline. I studied his powerful teachings for many years before we became personally connected through our mutual friend Todd McDonald when we shared the same publisher, American Media. By that time, I had also become friends with Zig Ziglar and become more closely connected to Paul Meyer, who were both my heroes. And as I learned more about goal-setting and applied the concepts to my own life, it started taking on a completely new dimension of success. I wanted to help other people find that new dimension, as well, and that's what led to the conception and publication of *Designing Your Own Life.*

When the tax laws changed and oil dropped to a fourth of its value in 1986, it took all my wealth with it, and boy did I experience a wakeup call. Have you ever been there? My goals really shifted from just wanting to *have* everything, to wanting to share, to experience, to give, and most importantly, to *become*. A big part of that shift in philosophy came from my study of Jim Rohn and his president (and my friend) Kyle Wilson. Jim and I eventually became colleagues, and I began emceeing his events, where I gained the life-changing realization that "becoming" is a goal. That shift can change your whole foundation of life, and I really drive that thinking home in this book.

I have set and refined my goals virtually every quarter of every year for forty years. That's four decades of refinement! My current goals now consist of almost 150 pages. One of the most important principles I learned through all my searching and studying is that you cannot truly be successful if you don't have a plan, and you cannot complete a good plan without setting goals with clear objectives. That's a principle I really hope you learn as well, as it is foundational to living a successful life.

What does the book say?

What makes this book so valuable is the distinction of finding clarity. Achieving a real understanding of your values—those things that are most important to you and that guide your life—leads to clarity of your purpose, which leads to a clearer vision of where you want to go in life. And that, of course, leads to setting and writing down the goals that will take you there. So, when you do the activities that support your goals (I call them *High Leverage Activities*, or HLAs), your goals align with your values, and your values support your purpose statement, chances are you'll get extraordinary results.

How will the book help you?

Here's a huge takeaway: One big piece of goal-setting that many people miss is the role the reticular activating system (RAS) plays in accomplishing your goals. The RAS is a set of nerves at the bottom of your brain that acts like a gatekeeper or sorting office. It evaluates and prioritizes all incoming information and determines what gets in and what gets your attention. Essentially, it allows what you need, want, or desire into your brain. Because your conscious brain can't capture everything, the more serious you are about what you want and focus on, the more your subconscious focuses on achieving it. When you set a goal, your RAS knows that's something you're really interested in, and it allows it to come in. When you understand that writing down and visualizing your goals activates your RAS, you can strategically use the power of your brain to help you reach your goals. In reality, most people don't set goals, and that may be because they lack an understanding of the RAS. (For more on RAS, see my YouTube video called "Tony Jeary on the Reticular Activating System.")

Since the reticular activating system filters those objectives you've written down as goals to come more often into your line of focus, you not only begin to see the goals in your mind; you also start to see things around you that will help you achieve your goals. If you don't write your goals down, then your brain likely doesn't recognize their importance, and your RAS may filter out things you might need to help you achieve them.

Another big piece to the goal-achieving puzzle is focusing on your own accomplishments. The more you do, the more you reinforce the fact that goals work. Did you raise great kids? Have you maintained good health? Do you have a healthy outlook on life? Do you have good habits? Have you traveled and seen many parts of the world? By focusing on whatever you've accomplished, you're allowing your RAS to prove that goal-setting works! (For more on why goal-setting works, see my YouTube video called "Tony Jeary on Why Goals Work—RAS.)

In *Designing Your Own Life*, we devoted a special area to accomplishments, broken down to the five areas of goal-setting—what you've accomplished in terms of having, what you've shared, what you've experienced, what you've been given, and what you've become.

For example, I listed in my "experienced" area of accomplishments that I've had a perfect 850 FICA score. It took me thirty years to figure out how to achieve this score, and it was a real accomplishment when I finally nailed it. I've also seen fifty countries, been on the commodities trading floor in New York, advised on the floor of the Senate in D.C., and overseen the wealth management of some two dozen families on the Forbes 400 Richest People in America list. When you write down your accomplishments, you propel your beliefs and fuel the achievement of your goals.

What have you experienced? What have you shared? What have you given? What have you become? And what do you have? List those accomplishments in each area so you'll have a better grasp of the power of goal-setting. Then set more goals in each of those five areas for the future. When those goals are tied to your purpose statement, which is tied to your values, your list of accomplishments will grow exponentially.

In the list of sixty values on the next page, identify the six to ten that best define what's most important to you. Those are the values that should be driving your goals in each of the five areas.

VALUES

1. Affection
2. Alignment
3. Altruism
4. Appearance
5. Appreciated
6. Attitude
7. Cleanliness
8. Congruence
9. Contentment
10. Cooperation
11. Creativity
12. Education
13. Effectiveness
14. Efficiency
15. Fairness
16. Faith
17. Fame
18. Family
19. Financial Security
20. Freedom
21. Friendship
22. Fun
23. Generosity
24. Genuineness
25. Happiness
26. Harmony
27. Health
28. Honesty
29. Humility
30. Inner Peace
31. Inspiration
32. Intimacy
33. Joy
34. Knowledge
35. Lifestyle
36. Loved
37. Loyalty
38. Motivation
39. Openness
40. Organization
41. Personal Brand
42. Personal Improvement
43. Personal Salvation
44. Philanthropy
45. Power
46. Productivity
47. Recognition
48. Respect
49. Results
50. Romance
51. Routine
52. Security
53. See the World
54. Simplicity
55. Solitude
56. Spiritual Maturity
57. Status
58. Wealth
59. Winning
60. Wisdom

BOOK 4
HOW TO GAIN 100
EXTRA MINUTES A DAY

The results you get are directly related to where and how you invest your time. This little book is packed with proven practices that can impact your time management and efficiency, both personally and professionally, and help you go to the next level of maximizing the minutes in your day.

I became intrigued by the subject of time management years ago after studying under Richard Clipp, who was a professional trainer and my mentor at the time. Since poor time management keeps many people from reaching their goals, my company TJI (Tony Jeary International) started making time management a foundational teaching early on to help our clients maximize the minutes in their busy schedules. How about you? How well do you strategically manage your time?

My original book on time management was called *Finding 100 Extra Minutes a Day*. Several years ago we updated that book and called it *How to Gain 100 Extra Minutes a Day*. The time-management distinctions in both books eventually led to the concept of MOLO (More of, Less of), my most well-known and well-used time management tool. It quickly and efficiently helps you audit for clarity what you want more of as well as what you less of. Then you can make adjustments by noting what you need to be doing more of and what you need to do less of with your time and effort. I encourage you to complete the MOLO matrix we've included at the end of this narrative for a serious look at where you can gain extra time in your life.

What does the book say?

Both books share the four-part time-management methodology called P.A.I.D.—**P**rioritize, **A**void Procrastination, **I**mprove Organizational Skills, and **D**elegate—four critical areas of time management that will dramatically improve your success.

How will the book help you?

We've included here four special audits that were in the original book that will help you become more aware of things you can do to actually save (or gain) 100 extra minutes a day.

Expanded Thinking

Since these books were written, I've realized that there's another big piece to the time puzzle: You should not only manage and save your time, you should also save and manage your energy. For example, you don't want to have time for your kids and yet have no energy to do anything with them. You need to have both.

Prioritizing Time-Gainer Audit

	Action	Average Minutes Gained/Saved in a Given Day
1	*Set priorities* during daily planning; eliminating unproductive tasks gains valuable time.	
2	Have *clear objectives and a written agenda* (and follow it) for every meeting, with no more than three objectives.	
3	*Learn to say no* to plans that don't benefit you, or send the request to the appropriate person.	
4	*Learn when your high-energy time is* and schedule your priority work for this time.	
5	*Prioritize your reading* by learning to skim articles, memos, books, etc. Then read only what really gives you value.	
6	Request that people who send you emails prioritize and *spell out the actions* they are asking of you, with clear bullet points, not long narratives.	
7	*Write down your objectives before you return phone calls* to gain time through quicker, more effective communication.	
8	Ask the originator of a document/email to send you *only the relevant information* that pertains to you.	
9	*Create lists often.* This helps with focus and multi-tasking.	
10	Prioritize and review the list of tasks you've given a subordinate.	
11	*Use the electronic calendar* to help prioritize daily events. Color-code by type of activity or level of priority.	
12	Control time-wasting activities.	
13	Other:	
14	Other:	
15	Other	
	Total time saved/gained in an average day:	

Procrastinator Time-Gainer Audit

	Action	Average Minutes Gained/Saved in a Given Day
1	*Identifying deadlines every morning* gains time and hinders procrastination.	
2	By identifying and *doing "little" things when you have open minutes waiting,* you will gain extra minutes later because they are already completed.	
3	*Making to-do lists and marking items off* as they are accomplished gains you valuable time later as you gain confidence and satisfaction in seeing things accomplished. This reduces possible procrastination.	
4	*Getting up X number of minutes earlier every day* can give you more productive time.	
5	Identify frequent tasks that you have already pro-crastinated on and *perform them way out in advance.*	
6	Gain valuable minutes by *starting the day's tasks quickly.* Do not ponder the difficulties of the day. Lay out your "first job" the night before.	
7	*Break one big task for this week (or month) into smaller, manageable parts* to help fight the tendency to procrastinate.	
8	*Stocking up on all supplies*—greeting cards, birthday cards, stamps, presents, etc.—gains extra minutes by not having to go shopping for them individually.	
9	Once an assignment has reached the "emergency" level, it has been procrastinated on. Identify future assignments and gain valuable time by *listing the tasks* needed to assure they won't become emergencies.	
10	*Preprinting cards and labels* for repetitive correspondence gains critical time every time you send one. Think about using macros and form letters on your computer.	
11	Other:	
12	Other:	
13	Other:	
	Total time saved/gained in an average day:	

Organizational Time-Gainer Audit:

	Action	Average Minutes Gained/Saved in a Given Day
1	*Keep a project by the phone to work on while talking.* However, make sure your conversation is not distracted, and only review as appropriate.	
2	*Listen to audio recordings* while you drive (or commute)—great for research.	
3	*Store things close to the place where they are used* (paper, supplies, etc.) to save time walking from one place to another.	
4	*Use a color-coded filing system* so you can find important papers and documents faster.	
5	*Double up on tasks.* (Find *Elegant Solutions*: exercise + reading = savings)	
6	*Combine errands* to gain time and increase productivity. Take a list with you.	
7	*Develop a "template" agenda* (an example is the 3-D Outline™ format taught in my book *Inspire Any Audience*) for meetings, and fine-tune it for every meeting.	
8	*Keep reading materials* with you to read while you are waiting in line, getting your car worked on, etc.	
9	For incoming mail, *provide screening guidelines* that keep the trivial away from you (if applicable).	
10	*When dealing with email, use the forward and delete keys freely.* Leverage your phone and your team (see my book, *Too Many Emails*).	
11	*Use prepackaged kits* for overnight travel. This will gain you the time it takes to pack these items.	
12	*Keep travel checklists on your phone* and keep one inside your suitcase to save time packing.	
13	Other:	
14	Other:	
15	Other:	
	Total time saved/gained in an average day:	

Delegation Time-Gainer Audit

	Event	Average Minutes Gained/Saved in a Given Day
1	*Trade projects with an associate* whose abilities and gifts fit the project better than yours.	
2	*Have a briefing* with someone you've delegated to and check the status so you don't have the responsibility for follow-up.	
3	*Utilize administrative personnel* to handle correspondence, filing, mailings, etc., when possible.	
4	*Use delivery (courier) and cleaning services* to free up your time to do what you do best. "Trade money for time."	
5	*Make a daily list of items that need to be accomplished* and determine if others can help you first thing each morning.	
6	*Contract outside services or consultants when no one in-house has the skills or capacity to perform the task.* This will gain you valuable time by not having to train and retrain someone.	
7	*Give enough detailed feedback* on projects so the recipient will be able to learn and increase their skills for the next project. This will gain you time in re-dos.	
8	*By delegating someone to extract the key points* from long reports, you will gain time as well as pertinent information, for faster, more effective results.	
9	*Have others read for you,* as well as highlight and recap for you.	
10	*Use Post-it Notes™ and/or email* to effectively delegate to others. A quick note can save valuable time if both people are not together for the handoff.	
11	*Audio record assignments* if you don't write well or have a driving trip where you can delegate.	
12	Other:	
13	Other:	
14	Other:	
	Total time saved/gained in an average day:	

Expanded Thinking

Since the original book was published, I've learned through years of bringing these concepts into cultures through webinars that most people don't have a frame of reference for how many hours they have to utilize in a given week. We've developed a model that shows my view of time.

We all have 168 hours in a week, and if you take out 56 hours for sleep (8 hours a night) and 12 hours for maintenance, that leaves 100 hours. Most people divide those 100 hours pretty evenly—50 for personal time and 50 for professional time. How well you strategically manage those 100 hours will determine your results.

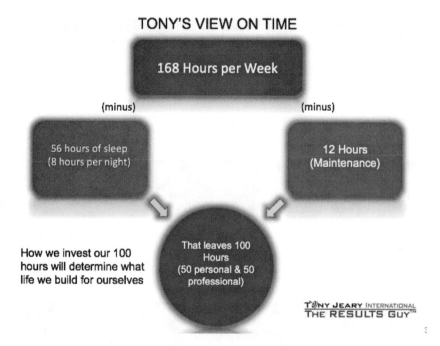

TONY'S VIEW ON TIME

168 Hours per Week

(minus)   (minus)

56 hours of sleep   12 Hours
(8 hours per night)   (Maintenance)

How we invest our 100   That leaves 100
hours will determine what Hours
life we build for ourselves (50 personal & 50
                           professional)

TONY JEARY INTERNATIONAL
THE RESULTS GUY™

MOLO (More Of ... Less Of)

What do we need to do more of?			
#	What	Why	Who
1			
2			
3			
4			

What do we need to do less of?			
#	What	Why	Who
1			
2			
3			
4			

What do we need to start doing?			
#	What	Why	Who
1			
2			
3			
4			

What do we need to stop doing?			
#	What	Why	Who
1			
2			
3			
4			

What do we need to do differently?			
#	What	Why	Who
1			
2			
3			
4			

BOOK 5
MEETING MAGIC

No other single action will enhance business efficiency and effectiveness more than consistent use of good meeting management techniques. The *Meeting Magic* formula leverages efficient use of time, enthusiastic participation, and respect for individuals and their views. *Meeting* Magic will untie your hands and help you get more effective, quality work done on time!

How do you rate your company's meeting effectiveness? If you think it could use improvement, this book will show you how to take strategic steps to bring that about.

Meeting Magic was the first of several books I wrote with my good friend George Lowe. When I was coaching the president of Ford, I got a call from them one day, and they said, "Tony, we would like for you to facilitate helping about two hundred of our top leaders work together more as a *High Performing Team*. I said, "I'm not a team-building expert." They said, "We'll give you a million dollars," and I said, "I will become one." They gave me a P.O. for $1,086,000, and I went out and researched the best team-building concepts and hired many of the best experts to teach me about team-building. I became an expert on the subject. (We'll talk more about *High-Performing Teams* in the narrative for Book 47, *Change—Mindset Matters*.)

When Ford gave me the assignment, though, they said, "We'll give you the contract for a million dollars; however, there is one thing you have to do." When I asked what that one thing was, they said, "You have to handle George Lowe." I asked, "Who is George Lowe?" "George is one of our top executives, who lives in San Francisco," they said, "and he's our tough nut to crack." I said, "I can handle him," and their response was, "Good luck!"

I flew out to California to meet with George and shared with him our plans for the team-building project. Just before the meeting was over, though, George got up and walked out of the meeting and his second-in-command took over. He went over to a flip chart, drew a line down the middle of the page, and put a plus sign on one side and a minus sign on the other. I had no idea what was going on. Then he started debriefing my meeting! He asked his team, "What went right in Tony's meeting today? And what could he improve?" As it turns out, that was a standard operating procedure for anyone who worked for George Lowe—to make sure every meeting was debriefed. I thought, *I like this guy!* Among the tens of thousands of people who worked for Ford, George was known as the "meeting policeman" (even though that was not his official position), and I really respected him for that. After working for George and getting to know him, I gained a tremendous amount of respect for his expertise.

Expanded Thinking

At the time *Meeting Magic* was published, the guidelines assumed the meeting leader was in charge because that was the guideline we had all "grown up with." I have since altered these guidelines and now teach that every attendee of a meeting is responsible for a meeting's success (i.e., all meeting participants should help the leader achieve winning outcomes). See my next book, *We've Got to Stop Meeting Like This*, which George and I wrote as a follow-up to *Meeting Magic*, for more details.

I went to him and said, "George, you're the meeting guy and I'm the presentation guy. Let's combine our know-how and write a book about how to have great meetings." And so we did.

What does the book say?

We came up with the mnemonic MAGIC for the five distinctions we wanted to drive home in the book:

Meet or Not Meet: Determine whether a meeting is the best way to accomplish your goal.

Agenda: With the end in mind (clear and written objectives), carefully build an agenda to make your objectives a reality. The big takeaway here is that the objectives trump the agenda (i.e., in most cases, the agenda should be fluid to ensure it can be adjusted as needed to reach the meeting's objectives).

Guidelines: Set and follow "the rules" that will allow you to conduct the meeting with confidence and success.

Involvement: Participate and encourage others to do the same. That is, after all, why you have meetings. Be sure you don't talk down to or talk "at" people. Get your audience engaged and involved, whether the meeting is by phone or the web or in person. (Involvement became the centerpiece for the IPRESENT model I introduced in my bestseller *Life is a Series of Presentations* years later. We'll talk more about involvement in the narrative for that book.)

Clarity: Communicate clearly to help ensure success.

In the back of the book are valuable forms to help you prepare for "magic" meetings—worksheets, checklists, and tips for how to use our famous 3-D Outline™ to develop the what, why, and how of the agenda. There are also meeting evaluation forms and tons more.

How will the book help you?

Based on polling tens of thousands of audience members from the stage around the globe, I have personally found that most people rate their organization's meeting effectiveness about a five, on a scale of one to ten. When we are commissioned by those companies to improve that number, we use this *Meeting Magic* model:

Meeting MAGIC

M — **Meet or Not?**
Decide that a meeting is the best tool for the job

A — **Agendas**
Documented and developed to support the objectives

G — **Guidelines**
Set expectations, protocol and how the meeting should operate

I — **Involvement**
Get and keep all the attendees engaged the entire meeting

C — **Clarity**
Clear communications throughout, including documents the actions agreed upon

Expanded Thinking

Another piece to this distinction is clarity of action. When you and the other participants walk away from the meeting, you want to do so with everyone knowing exactly what actions each person is to take. That way, people can take ownership of their assignments and be held accountable for making things happen. In meetings with my clients, we use a TJI notes template (email us at info@tonyjeary.com if you would like a copy), on which we clearly document the actions to take and who is responsible for each.

Additionally, we help organizations develop guidelines and standards from the core ten below, which we delve into further in Book 38, *We've Got to Start Meeting and Emailing Like This:*

1. Have a clear purpose and defined objective(s) for every meeting.
2. Ensure that the right people are either in the room, on the phone, or represented.
3. Create *and follow* a realistic, timed agenda.

4. Start and end the meeting on time.
5. Acknowledge that achieving winning outcomes is not just the meeting leader's responsibility but everyone's responsibility.
6. Facilitate for results so that everyone stays involved and engaged.
7. Take thorough notes, documenting important discussion points, outcomes, and agreements.
8. Develop a "who does what by when" action plan.
9. Publish meeting notes and action plans quickly and follow up to ensure timely execution.
10. Strategically cascade meeting outcomes promptly and consistently to others in the organization.

My professional life is spent mostly in my studio in meetings with executives and teams. My staff is carefully trained to implement every one of the above points. Notes of critical points are displayed on a large screen for all to see and comment on. Meeting notes usually go out to participants within minutes of the meeting's adjournment. I can't tell you how often I hear comments like "If we can get our meeting to run as smoothly as this one, we will have made great strides."

BOOK 6
WE'VE GOT TO STOP
MEETING LIKE THIS

We've Got to Stop Meeting Like This provides simplified meeting
management distinctions for *both* meeting leaders and participants.

This was the second book I authored with my friend George
Lowe. By this time, George and I had changed our paradigm from the
"old school" thinking we had grown up with (i.e., that the meeting
leader was solely responsible for the outcome of the meeting). We
had transitioned to the concept that participants can help make the
meeting more successful when they take ownership of it, as well. This
book goes deeper with these and other best practices from Book 5,
Meeting Magic, our first book together.

Around the time we wrote this book, I was coaching the
president of Firestone, and he said to me, "I'm in charge of factories,
distribution, roofing products, and more, and we need our meetings
to be impactful at all levels." He commissioned TJI to customize
five standards for Communication Mastery within Firestone and to

cascade our meeting effectiveness standards down to thousands of his people, all their factories, and even down to the shop safety meeting level.

How committed are you to changing the meeting culture of your company? If a company like Firestone can transform their meeting culture from top to bottom, couldn't it happen for your company as well? This book will help you change your thinking so you can reap the benefits of disciplined meetings with valuable outcomes.

What does the book say?

If you answer yes to any of the following questions, then the ideas contained in this book can save you time and money and help your team or organization become more effective:

1. Do you believe your meetings frequently are not an effective use of your time?
2. Do you work for or with people who are not sensitive to the costs related to meetings?
3. Have you attended meetings recently that created more problems than they solved?
4. Have you ever found it hard to get a word in edgewise or felt like putting a gag on someone who dominated a meeting?
5. Do you recognize that meetings can be a great showcase for leadership and management talents and can help you really execute when utilized effectively?

This book is full of useful ideas on preparing for and conducting your meetings and even includes templates to show you the best room layouts for the various sizes and types of meetings. In the Appendix, there are handy forms for your use, including a meeting preparation checklist and a sample meeting announcement, agenda, and evaluation form as well as a section on troubleshooting.

How will the book help you?

The biggest takeaway is the paradigm shift from the meeting leader taking full ownership of the meeting to the need for both leaders and participants to own the meeting and help make it successful.

At the end of each chapter, there's a review featuring the chapter's highlights for the reader to complete. We've included information from two of the chapter reviews here to give you the benefit of those highlights.

Chapter One: Knowing What Success Looks Like

1. Just a <u>10 percent</u> reduction in time spent in meetings would result in substantial savings for organizations and improved work life for employees, so get serious about this subject.

2. For many in the workplace today, time has become <u>more</u> valuable than money. Make your minutes count!

3. Four things you should consider when determining whether or not a meeting is required:
    *   Results needed
    *   Type of work to be done
    *   Costs associated with the meeting
    *   Alternative methods available (to reach results needed)

4. Key alternatives to a face-to-face meeting are:
    *   Video or teleconferencing
    *   Online meetings
    *   Videotaped messages
    *   Paper or email bulletins with response mechanisms

5. Culture acceptance is important. Think: What does "critical mass" mean in relation to meeting management? Critical mass means you have to have enough people that "know the rules" of meeting management in order to get started and have at least some degree of management support. (The more the better. Think about how committed the president of Firestone was.)

6. Don't be too heavy on "meeting police." Meeting management is about achieving desired outcomes, not just getting done in an hour, regardless of results. Too stringent enforcement of rules at the expense of accomplishments can be counterproductive.

Chapter Two: Preparation Pays

1. Here are six key questions to consider as you prepare for a meeting:

    - *Who* should participate?
    - *What* do you want to accomplish?
    - *When* should you hold the meeting, and how long should it take?
    - *Where* should the meeting take place—in person, over the phone, etc.?
    - *Why* are you holding the meeting?
    - *How* should you conduct the meeting?

2. Purpose statements are short, punchy phrases that typically describe the <u>subject matter</u> content of a meeting. Desired outcome statements are longer and more specific—they describe the <u>actual work</u> to be accomplished during the session.

3. Generally speaking, a smaller group size is better if a high degree of interaction is needed.

4. There are many methods/techniques you can employ when conducting a meeting, such as:

    - Presentation
    - Present and discuss
    - Q&A
    - Brainstorm
    - Consolidate
    - Order/Prioritize
    - Develop
    - Agree
    - Evaluate
    - Recap

5. List desired outcomes or objectives at the top of a meeting agenda or next to the topics.

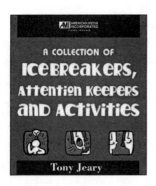

BOOK 7
A COLLECTION OF ICEBREAKERS, ATTENTION KEEPERS, AND ACTIVITIES

Icebreakers is a book of exercises and breakouts that will help you break the ice when you're giving a talk, a webinar, a training, or any other type of presentation. With the exercises we developed and gathered, you can create an environment where your audience members feel more comfortable accepting new ideas, taking risks, and really listening to and absorbing your message. When you engage your audience, you can be assured they pay closer attention to what you're saying, enjoy it more, and walk away with a lot more takeaways from the information you've given them.

When we wrote the book, I was running TJI (Tony Jeary International) more as a large international training company and was focused as a two-tier supplier to eight different multinational communication and advertising agencies. We needed a book that was designed to improve trainers' ability to connect with their audience and gain involvement. As you can tell by now, I'm a big component of involvement, so I wanted to create a book that listed easy activities you could do to interact and engage with your audience. *Icebreakers* turned out to be a bestseller through our catalog sales for seven or eight years.

My friend Todd McDonald was actually the one who came up with the idea for the book. You may remember that he was the publisher for American Media, who was also publishing for Brian Tracy at the time, and the American Media relation produced a lifelong friendship for the two of us. I had been studying Brian's works for years, and my relationship with him went from just a mentor from afar to true colleagues, and eventually to an even more personal level as mutually respected friends.

Here's a quick story: I called Brian one day years ago and asked him how much he would charge me to come to my private studio and invest a day in coaching me. He said he would be glad to come for no charge. I was a bit shocked! I asked if we could at least send him a first-class ticket, and he said, "No, I'll pay my own way." Then I asked if we could have my driver pick him up, and he said, "Sure."

He came here to my *Strategic Acceleration* studio, coached me for a day, and poured into me. As I was riding with him and my driver on the way back to the airport, I asked him why he would invest a day of his life helping me like he did. I'll always remember his words: "You have a great mind, Tony, and I wanted to tap into it." I was so humbled to hear that from such a great authority in the industry whom I had looked up to, followed, studied, and been mentored by like very few others. We certainly went to a deeper level of relationship that day.

Have you ever thought about having a great expert whose works you admire come in and mentor you? After investing a day with someone of renowned authority, I can pretty much guarantee you will never be the same. It's a great way to up your game—something we should always be doing.

What does the book say?

Icebreakers has more than 100 exercises and interactive activities to help you set just the right tone for your presentation. Here is a sample exercise from each of the four categories:

Openers and Icebreakers

(The most important part of your presentation may be the first three minutes. The activities in this section might be the very key you're looking for to give you that "wow" factor right off the bat.)

Introduce Me

What: An activity that illustrates how meaningful—but often inaccurate—first impressions can be; it's also a humorous icebreaker for training seminars, where most participants are strangers to one another.

How:

1. Before participants are introduced to one another, have them sit in a large circle. Inform the attendees that instead of introducing themselves, they will introduce the person sitting on their right. This should cause some murmuring in the crowd, since most people will not know a thing about one another.

2. The individual making the introduction should guess a first name, job, hobbies, and family situation (married, single, kids, pets, etc.) for their neighbor on the right. After the "guesswork" introduction is complete, the neighbor should accurately introduce her/himself.

3. Continue until all participants have been introduced.

Discussion:

1. What does this activity say about first impressions? What do we base first impressions on?

2. What are stereotypes? What do we make them? Do you sometimes avoid meeting people based on stereotypes?

3. Who feels more comfortable with the group now? Are you likely to remember each other's names and introductions better with this activity than you would with a simple, "Hi, my name is_____" activity?

Materials:

None

Time required:
>Roughly two minutes per participant.

Attention Keepers and Energizers

(It's very important to keep your audience energized. In this section you'll find games, brainteasers, mental "warm-ups," and a variety of unique and fun crowd energizers.)

Did You Catch All That?

What: A quick brainteaser that illustrates the need to listen carefully and follow directions closely.

How:
1. Distribute blank sheets of paper to the audience members. Tell them they will be given two tasks to do, and they must try and perform them very quickly. Inform them that they will only hear the directions once.

Task #1: Ask them to spell out two words from these letters: OODRWWTS. They can only use the letters the number of times they have been said, and they must use all the letters.

Task #2: Ask them to give the letter of the alphabet that would logically follow this sequence of letters: OTTFFSS.

Answers:

Task #1: "Two words"

Task #2: "E" for "eight." (The first letters of numbers one through seven make up the given sequence.)

2. Give the answers.

Closing Activities

(This section will give you just the right way to emphasize that final point and create great closure at the end of the day, so your participants will leave with your best takeaways at the top of their mind.)

Rapid Review

What: A chance to review key concepts during a session; a method of testing the learning/retention capacity of your group.

How:
1. Immediately before or just after a break or lunchtime, tell participants that you want to do a brief review. Ask participants to call out things they learned. Set a number and say, for example, "I want to hear ten of the concepts/ideas you learned!" to get the audience moving quickly.
2. Repeat this procedure before or after breaks throughout the session. You may want to jot these items down on a board or a flip chart that you keep in view throughout the day.

Discussion:
>   None needed.

Materials:
>   Flip chart or board

Time required:
>   About fifteen minutes several times throughout the day.

Quotes of the Pros

(Looking for just the right quote to accentuate a point? You'll find them in this section.)

>   Most conversations are just alternating monologues.
>   The question is, is there any real listening going on?
>
>   —Leo Buscaglia

>   The quality of any product or service is
>   what the customer says it is.
>
>   —James Balkcom

>   Any business arrangement that is not profitable to
>   the other fellow will, in the end, prove unprofitable
>   to you. The bargain that yields mutual satisfaction
>   is the only one that is apt to be repeated.
>
>   —B. C. Forbes

For easy access, each of the four categories is organized by these subcategories:

- Communication
- Customer Service
- Diversity
- Leadership
- Quality
- Sales
- Managing Stress
- Team Building
- Time Management
- Train the Trainer
- Generic

How will the book help you?

Even the most charismatic speaker could use some tips on jazzing up a presentation or talk, whether it's to an audience of five hundred people or to a staff of five employees. *Icebreakers* is your handy reference guide filled with exercises and activities to break the ice, engage with your audience, hold their attention, and support any type of presentation.

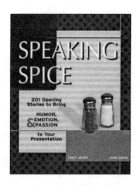

BOOK 8
SPEAKING SPICE

Speaking Spice, a companion book to *Icebreakers,* is a collection of 201 opening stories and one-liners that can help you bring humor, emotion, and passion to your presentations.

Early on, I realized the importance of helping clients inject a little humor into their presentations. Everyone needs to become more strategic about using what I call *Business Entertainment*—one of the Seven Foundational Secrets® I drive home in my book *Inspire Any Audience. Business Entertainment* is that appropriate fun factor that brings greater impact and enhances virtually any presentation.

For me, there was only one problem—at that time I wasn't really a very funny person! So in my search for a strategic solution, I went to the Comedy Gym, a spinoff of Improv, to learn more about humor. I discovered that there are about eight major ways to bring humor into a presentation. Two of the most effective methods are telling jokes to make people laugh (and I'm still not good at that) or facilitating humor to both make people laugh *and* bring involvement. I knew I could do that! I quickly came up with the idea of giving away one-dollar bills during my presentations to egg people on when they make a humorous remark. That way, I let the people who *are* funny interject the humor into my presentation for me, and it's worked remarkably well. It ensures that people laugh, and I get great involvement from my audience, which enhances the experience.

It's also a great idea to use funny videos in your presentations as a way of inputting the smile factor and giving you what I've coined as a *Breathing Space*. That's actually one of the big takeaways from the IPRESENT model I introduce in *Life is a Series of Presentations*, my thirty-first book.

Knowing there were probably other people out there like me who had more or less missed the humor gene, my team and I went on a search to find and collect funny stories that would help alleviate that stressor for them. The result was *Speaking Spice*.

What does the book say?

As I was researching humor, I discovered that only 10 percent of the people in the world can tell a joke with a good punch line—one out of ten. *Speaking Spice* was written with that in mind. So if you're like me and can't tell good jokes, the more than 200 stories and one-liners in this book will support you in making people laugh in your presentations. It's a way of strategically connecting with your audience and creating an atmosphere for trust and buy-in, something I reinforce in several of my books—*Inspire Any Audience, Speaking from the Top,* and *Life is a Series of Presentations.*

How will the book help you?

The easy-to-use table of contents shows the time it takes to share the story as well as the category (attitude, motivation, perseverance, results, leadership, or general) and the mood (serious, humorous, emotional, or thoughtful) for each story. With those descriptors, you can quickly find just the right one for your presentation.

Of course, there's Google as well. Whether you use Google or reference books like *Speaking Spice*, I encourage you to strategically search for and discover just the right content that will help you make a great presentation and deliver on your objectives.

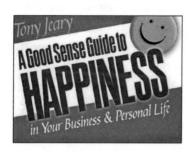

BOOK 9
A GOOD SENSE GUIDE
TO HAPPINESS

Managing our busy lives can be quite a challenge for all of us. In *A Good Sense Guide to Happiness*, you'll discover encouraging and resourceful ways to strategically create a more abundant and fruitful life, both personally and professionally. Each easy-to-read nugget is packed with a wealth of wisdom and some good old-fashioned common sense to help you increase your happiness in all areas of your life.

As I met and worked with many people all over the world in the early years of my vocation, I became intrigued with the idea of happiness. I started noting the distinctions that lead to living a happy and successful life and became especially captivated with the whole idea of the difference between joy and happiness. (Joy is a deep inner peace that is not affected by changing circumstances. Happiness is based on external happenings and is most often temporary. In this book, though, I use "happiness" and "joy" interchangeably because most people are more familiar with the concept of happiness.) That prompted me to start studying the concept of happiness, and I've continued studying over the years to the point that I've become somewhat of an expert on the subject. In fact, I've just finished writing what has now become my fiftieth book, *Living Life Smiling*, which goes into much more depth about joy and happiness and gives strategic distinctions for living a happy life.

What does the book say?

The book is full of powerful quotes and tips for nurturing, practicing, and finding happiness. We include specific, strategic advice for finding happiness:

- In your career
- In your finances
- Through your accomplishments
- Through your organizational skills
- Through your knowledge
- Through your good communication
- Through your good health
- As a manager
- As a presenter

Here are a few examples:

From the "Finding Happiness in Your Career" section:

"Strive for excellence. There's nothing more satisfying than the feeling you get from doing something well. Most people have average abilities in a wide variety of interests, and yet each of us is able to achieve distinction in at least one specific activity. Make an effort to find and develop your personal area of excellence."

From the "Finding Happiness in Your Finances" section:

"Never love money. Money is not evil. It's the love of money that's the root of all evil. If you become too attached to money, it becomes too hard to make. Learn to save it and also learn to give it. Know the playing field and the rules of the game. Then you can share in the winning trophy with the rest of the team."

From the "Finding Happiness as a Presenter" section:

"Use the 20/20/20 rule. Those who are listening will make a judgment about you and your remarks within the first twenty seconds—what you nonverbally communicate in the twenty square inches around your face and shoulders and the first twenty words out of your mouth. Begin with confidence. They want you to succeed."

How will the book help you?

I preach, teach, and live the idea that being strategic in everything you do will help you get extraordinary results, and finding happiness is no exception. When you strategically search for and then implement ways to bring happiness into every area of your life, you'll be amazed at the results. And this principle applies to everyone, whether you're a skilled craftsman or a high-powered executive. I think you'll treasure this powerful collection that will guide you down the path of true success in all areas of your life.

BOOK 10
SUCCESS ACCELERATION

If success in your personal or professional life seems like an elusive and unattainable dream, this collection of principles for strategically achieving success can provide the motivation you need for a breakthrough. *Success Acceleration* provides solutions to many of the pitfalls that often hinder success and even shows you how to accelerate the process.

This book turned out to be a magical book for Amway because it spoke so powerfully to the person in the field (MLM, direct sales reps, etc.) who were hungry to grow. In fact, it was so successful in helping their people grow to the next level that they would often order twenty to twenty-five thousand of these books at a time. The book was and still is a hit. I share the principles almost weekly.

What does the book say?

By reading, studying, and listening to the greatest experts on success and achievement in the world for many years—including Og Mandino, Napoleon Hill, Norman Vincent Peale, Zig Ziglar, Earle

Nightingale, Brian Tracy, and many others—I began to develop my own ideas and strategies about success and personal achievement. I found certain "shortcuts" to success and discovered that some achievement principles were more effective than others. I realized that some foundational principles actually drive and support other success factors and that the learning curve for acquiring and utilizing success principles can be quickened.

The key—which is the premise of *Success Acceleration*—is that the process of achieving success can be expedited *if you are willing to open your mind and actually change if you need to.* If you're not willing to change, you will not better yourself. It's that simple. When your willingness to change connects with the right success principles and action steps, the inevitable result is an acceleration of your personal achievement.

In this book we discuss the three key segments in the process of success acceleration:

- Foundations
- Strategies
- Tactics

If you can truly understand why you do the things you do (establish your foundation), become aware of the things you need to do (build your strategy) and change your actions accordingly (apply the tactics), you can quicken personal achievement.

How will the book help you?

Over the years I've come to realize that models are the fastest way to learn virtually anything. In this book, I introduce into my work for the first time two popular models: the concept of the *Belief Window* and my own concept of *Production Before Perfection* (PBP). These two powerhouse models will change your thinking forever and accelerate your success more than you can imagine.

The concept of the *Belief Window* has been around for a long time—since the 1920s, in fact. A guy by the name of Hyrum Smith, who was Stephen Covey's partner, began making it popular about twenty years ago. After I discovered his version of it on an audio, I listened to it dozens of times.

The *Belief Window* concept complements and supports the paradigm model—one made popular by a client of mine by the name of Joel Barker. Joel wrote a book called *Paradigms: The Business of Discovering the Future*, and also developed a powerful video (at one time, it was the most watched training video ever) called "The Business of Paradigms." I've been fascinated for years with both Hyrum Smith's and Joel Barker's teachings, which are all about uncovering your *Blind Spots*, and I've made that one of my foundational teachings, as well. (See both my YouTube video called "Tony Jeary on the Belief Window" and Joel Barker's two-minute YouTube video called "New Business of Paradigms: Second Edition with Joel Barker.")

We all have paradigms and principles on our *Belief Window* through which we filter life and process information. We begin forming the truisms or principles on our *Belief Window* right after birth, and we add to it the principles and truisms we accept and build our lives around as we get older. The principles on our *Belief Window* affect everything we see, hear, and experience, and consequently they affect the choices we make. Unless you're operating your life with flawless principles, you're probably not achieving the level of success you could. Have you ever thought about that? Uncovering the *Blind Spots* that reveal the flawed and/or outdated principles on your *Belief Window* can often catapult you toward quickening your achievement! Faulty principles = faulty results, and accurate principles = better results.

Production Before Production (PBP) ties into the *Belief Window* model and is one of my most famous concepts. Perhaps nothing prohibits achievement more than procrastination, and the belief that everything has to be just right or even perfect before you can begin is the foundational piece to why so many people procrastinate. The main idea of PBP is to take action first and get it perfect later, as you progress. It's one of the best antidotes for procrastination there is.

Procrastination is all about how you think and what your self-talk is. People who procrastinate often tell themselves one of these five things:

1. I can do it tomorrow.

2. I don' have everything I need, so I'll wait.
3. I can't do it perfectly, so I'll wait.
4. I don't have time right now.
5. Someone else can do it better.

Do you ever say any of those things to yourself?

In a major CBS special I made in 2009 (see the YouTube video called "Tony Jeary – TXA Channel 21 News on Procrastination"), I talked about the fact that there are both good and bad procrastination. Saying *I'll make a decision tomorrow* could be a good thing, because you may be intentionally allowing your intuition to think about it before you decide. However, if you say something like, *Everything's not quite perfect, so I don't think I'm going start on it yet,* and you don't take any action, then you're more than likely procrastinating because of your perfectionism. (See my YouTube video called "Positive and Negative Procrastination.")

My philosophy, which I sell every day to executives who commission my TJI firm to drive it into their organization, is execute to completion—get it done *now,* and get it done quickly. That's the best pathway to your *Success Acceleration!*

BOOK 11
HAPPY FAMILIES

If you want some great, yet simple ideas on how to grow and expand happiness in your life, read *Happy Families*. My daughter Brooke and I collaborated on this book when she was eight years old to bring you interesting ideas that could impact your family's happiness.

I have two daughters, three years apart, and Brooke is the oldest. When both Brooke and Paige reached the age of eight, I helped them become published authors so they could experience doing radio interviews and autographing, and so they could have perspective about what their dad did as an author. (We'll talk next about Paige's book— *Fun Things to Do as Kids*.) Brooke authored her second book, *Toned Bodies for Teens*, when she was sixteen, and Paige authored her second book, *Friendship*, when she was twelve. Later in life, having "published author of two books" on their resumes supported their confidence, uniqueness, and personal brands.

What does the book say?

It's a book full of ideas for activities that families could do together. Although it's written on a child's level, we encourage anyone— whether you are six, eight, twelve, or an adult—to read the book and keep it handy for ideas to do together as a family, any time or anywhere.

It starts with the definition of a happy family. A happy family is…

- A family who looks for the best in each other
- A family who looks for nice thing to do for each other
- A family who supports each other
- A family who laughs, cries, and prays together
- A family who makes happy memories together.

Then it gives a wealth of ideas for families to do when they:

- Have Fun Together
- Love, Care, and Give
- Worship Together
- Celebrate Together
- Learn Together
- Stick Together
- Laugh Together
- Make Happy Families (Happy Children Become Happy Parents)

How will the book help you?

If family happiness is a top priority for you (and it should be), you will enjoy this book. It also makes a great gift for children or even for other parents who want ideas for things to do with their kids.

Let me note one more idea for you: If you can, do what I did— find a way to share your profession/hobbies/special connections with your kids. Co-authoring these two books added to my connection with my daughters. Look for ways every day to do that with your kids.

BOOK 12
FUN THINGS TO DO AS KIDS

Kids just want to have fun! This is the book Paige and I co-authored when she was eight to give parents and kids great ideas for doing just that. We had tons of fun just writing the book together. In fact, as Paige's dad, it obviously gave me great joy to do so.

What does the book say?

Kids can have fun...

- With other people (or their dogs!)
- When playing sports
- When playing games
- When going places
- When serving others

How will the book help you?

Have fun with you kids, no matter their age. My mom and dad modeled that so well. If you're a parent, I encourage you to model it for your kids, as well. Kids will never say, "My parents were just too darned fun." It won't happen.

You can read this book yourself to get great ideas about ways your kids can have fun, or you can share it with your friends and family. Either way, we hope it makes you smile more and have more fun!

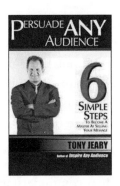

BOOK 13
PERSUADE ANY AUDIENCE

Life is a Series of Presentations is my thirty-first book, published with Simon & Schuster. I believe we're presenting hundreds of times a day, almost every time we interact with someone. Wouldn't you agree, though, that life is also a series of persuasions? Most, if not all, of our presentations are persuasive in nature. The ability to persuade other people to accept your products, services, or even ideas is critical to your success, in both your business and in your personal life.

If you're a person who is able to execute well, then you're obviously better than good at getting other people to help you—you know how to persuade and influence. Sadly, many people go through life and fail to strategically polish those skills. Which group are you in?

Everyone—whether their primary objective is to sell, persuade, or influence—should study persuasion, and study it on an ongoing basis. Do you want to persuade your kids to be exceptional in school? If you understand persuasion, chances are you could influence them to up their game a little as a student so they could have a great résumé and go out and be even more successful in life. If you're a manager, don't you want to be able to get your team to execute? Sure you do. Just think of all the benefits top-notch persuasion skills could bring to your life. All roles in life require you to persuade people to do something. With the right skill sets, you can better persuade any audience, whether it's one-on-one or a large group or somewhere in between.

Really, this is a prime example of how changing your thinking can change your results. When you understand the power of persuasion and strategically set out to improve your persuasion effectiveness, I believe you'll see both your personal and professional results skyrocket.

What does the book say?

By taking an hour to read this little book, you could gain six powerhouse techniques that will help you influence any audience.

How will the book help you?

We've included a template of the six simple, yet powerful steps that will help you persuade your audience. Each step has actions for the best execution. Although they are geared toward selling, these actions can certainly be applied to any type of persuasion or influence objective.

Step 1: Preparation Pays Big Dividends

1	Know your objective(s)	• Is the objective clearly understood?
2	Know what you are offering	• Product or service (define the real value/ benefit or loss they might avoid)
3	Study feedback from previous presentations	• If you don't have feedback, get it. • Why did they buy/say yes in the past?

(Continued)

4	"Juke box" of stories of past client situations	• Categorize and have ready success stories to pull from that apply to your current prospect. • Collect reference letters and stories in hardcopy and have them mentally ready.
5	Use quotes effectively	• Enhance your influence with trust transference using a well-known person's quote that supports your direction.
6	The sale starts with the first contact	• Do everything you can to be invited in. • Listening and taking "quote notes" help focus you and your team.
7	Insert a packaged kit or gift ahead of time	• Evoke the reciprocal principle with a gift of some kind up front.
8	Do your homework	• Learn the person/organization; ask questions of the prospect or people who have worked with the prospect—*anyone* who may have information. • Put your CIA hat on. • Study their marketing collateral. • Don't forget the receptionists and the executive assistants.
9	Getting to know your prospect/ audience member(s)	• Remember the individual's needs and wants. What personal benefit can they derive from your product or service? Promotion? Personal development? Brownie points?

(Continued)

10	**Seven subconscious desires of your audience**	• To belong • To be respected • To be liked • To be safe • To succeed • To find romance • To be inspired (enthused)
11	**Know the prospect's pain**	• Write it down. • Search out the *real* pain—the pain behind the pain.
12	**The REAL buyer**	• User buyers • Economic buyers—ability to get check written • Who is the real decision maker? • Organization chart—have prospect draw • Where does the prospect fit in?
13	**What's their budget?**	• Avoid overselling and underselling. • Sell to their point of need *at* their budget. • If not within realm—what's the point? • Can they combine budgets of two departments?
14	**Getting the contact—when and where**	• Location: yours, theirs or neutral • Home turf advantage
15	**The role of a team leader**	• Avoid consensus for consensus sake. • Procrastination hurts—bust through
16	**Rehearsing**	• In front of others • Video your pitch
17	**Hire a personal coach**	• Role model • Continuous improvement—benchmark internally

Step 2: Developing Your Pitch

18	**Visualize success**	• Mentally walk through each step of the pitch, including possible scenarios and different questions the prospect may ask.
19	**Have clear written objectives**	• Consider the objectives for the pitch *and* the bigger picture—prospect's personal agenda, company mission, future business, etc.
20	**It's not so much what you say ...**	• Body language, tone setting, and mechanics of the pitch make a difference. • 93 percent of communication is non-verbal. • Most people spend too much time on slides and not enough on body language.
21	**Weigh logic vs. emotion**	• Never underestimate the value of emotion in the buying decision.
22	**Start now, fix it later**	• Make it easy on yourself; get ideas and points down in an outline *now*. You can perfect them as the process develops. • Don't procrastinate. • Brainstorm ideas to get down on paper.
23	**3-D Outline™**	• 1st dimension = "What" • 2nd dimension = "Why" • 3rd dimension = "How" • Bonus dimensions = "Time" and "Who"
24	**Visual aids**	• Many people seem to put a lot of effort into the content of aids like PowerPoint; remember to vary your media and to ensure the environment supports you. • Use multi-media if possible. • Limitations/possibilities
25	**Photos**	• Most people are visual.

(Continued)

26	**Slides**	• Know your options (paper, 35mm, PowerPoint) • Audience size makes a difference. • Most appropriate—don't be too slick!
27	**Create curiosity**	
28	**Don't discount props**	• Make sure they are appropriate and applicable.
29	**Setting the environment**	• Value of arriving early • Set the room to your advantage.
30	**Quote notes**	• Take down their *exact* words and be sure to use them in communication back to them. People have a tough time objecting to their own words.
31	**The art of facilitation**	• The audience members are often the experts. • They often have the answers. • You are a guide—you are aware, not in control. • Staying out of the limelight can contribute to success.
32	**Be congruent**	• Body language • Tonality • Words
33	**Deal with integrity**	• Be real.

Step 3: Opening with Strength

34	**Targeted polling**	• Continue gathering intelligence and adjust if necessary, right to the minute you go on. • Create champions in the audience. • Use *Peer Trust Transference*.

(Continued)

35	Rapport (before, during, and after)	• Find commonalities (like we do when we first meet someone). Talk commonalities all the time.
36	Introductions	• Take advantage of *Trust Transference* by having an audience member introduce you; often even coach them with bullets.
37	The power of an opening	• Grab their attention.
38	Set up guidelines for optimum success	• Get agreement up front for how you expect things to flow.
39	Music	• If it's easy and appropriate, music adds a great deal to the "feel" of the pitch.
40	Match audience expectations	• Include a point in the very beginning to verbally survey the audience to confirm their expectations of the agenda, results, and important items. Be ready to adjust emphasis to the things that are most important to them.
41	Reconfirm agenda	• Gives permission for you to drive the meeting based on the agenda. • There is power in shifting the agenda on the fly—it shows you are in control of the pitch.
42	Prove you are ready	• Take 30 seconds to share with your audience what you did to prepare. • "In order to save time..." (Be careful not to sound arrogant.)
43	Eliminate the four audience tensions	• Pitch maker and team • Materials • Environment • Others in the room

(Continued)

44	**Create an agenda**	• Post and/or distribute for visual awareness • Use subdividers in PowerPoints slides • Summarize
45	**Materials**	• Make them engaging.
46	**Don't be too polished**	• You can be • Be good; don't be perfect.
47	**Make a positive first impression**	• Smile • Dress • Use people's names

Step 4: Managing Your Pitch

48	**Enthusiasm**	• Bring your energy to the table.
49	**Own the environment**	• Make adjustments on the fly. • Ask audience permission, but show benefits of adjustments. • Flip chart, projector, room temperature
50	**Set guidelines**	• Based on agreed-upon expectations, agendas, and timing • License to control • Renegotiate with audience—show you respect their time
51	**Use *Business Entertainment***	• Make time for appropriate doses of entertainment value. • Vary the media. • Relieve tension and get people to like you by association. • Use stories/anecdotes.
52	**Verbal survey**	• Monitor audience response during presentation.

(Continued)

53	**Team presenting**	• Starts with how you introduce your team members and correctly use their background and expertise to meet objectives • Think ahead of time about information that applies to your audience.
54	**Are you first or last in line?**	• Know where you are in line and adjust accordingly.
55	**Champions in the audience**	• Pre-meeting calls and targeted polling • Testimonials everywhere
56	**Use pauses**	• Position them effectively.
57	**Use strategic movement**	• Presenter movement • Anchor spots • Flip chart, story boards, etc.
58	**Don't use a lectern/podium**	• It separates you from the audience.
59	**Transitions/ pre-summary**	• Summarize after each key point and link to the next point.
60	**Q&A**	• Avoid the mistake of staging one big Q&A at the end. • Strategically plan and manage Q&As throughout. • Establish system of notes and/or HUHY (Help Us Help You).
61	**Handling objections**	• Note them
62	**Planned Spontaneity**	• The better prepared you are, the more spontaneity you can bring. • Enables you to give impromptu responses
63	**Listen more, talk less**	

Step 5: Closing Right

64	Summarize	• Highlight the discussion to each key point. • Lead into the actual close.
65	Pre-close	• Test with lines like "What should we do?"
66	Assume the close	• Future pace—look to the future and come back to the present. • Define the next step.
67	Communicate the value to them personally	• Keep communicating the value they're looking for. • If people get the feeling you need the money, you're dead. People buy because it will help them, not you.

Step 6: Follow Up

68	Win the pitch after the pitch	• Follow up with something of value to the buyer.
69	Make it easier on the customer	• Be easy to do business with. • Develop systems that work for you and for your customer.
70	The art of upselling	• Ask for a little extra.
71	Write a report (or two)	• Written summary of agreement • Status reports

BOOK 14
PRESENTING WITH STYLE

Have you ever given an entire presentation to someone, only to realize they didn't receive it well? Even though we live in a high-tech, instant-message world, we're still people working with people, each with a variety of personality styles. As you build relationships, whether for personal or professional reasons, it's important to understand people's personality style so you'll be better able to communicate with them in a style they're best able to receive it.

Co-authoring *Presenting with Style* with my good friend Dr. Robert Rohm was an amazing experience for me. Robert had created a big following in Amway over the years, and he became one of the world's most well-known experts on DISC Personality Profiling. We decided to put a book together using my presentation expertise and his DISC profile and assessment expertise.

What does the book say?

What's important is to present to people the way they want to receive it, versus just how you want to deliver it. Adjust your presentation style to their preferences, rather than vice versa. This applies whether you're presenting to your kids, your spouse, a prospect, an employee, a large or small group, or anyone else.

How will the book help you?

The DISC Model of Human Behavior helps you better understand the people you present to so you can give them the information in the way they would like to receive it. Here's the model:

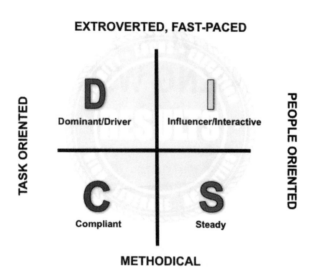

There are many personality profiles and assessments available today. This particular assessment has been around a long time, and it's simple because it's based on just two questions:

1. Are you more fast-paced or methodical?
2. Are you more people-oriented or task-oriented?

Look at the four quadrants in the model above. If you're fast-paced and task-oriented, you're in the "D" quadrant (Drive). Ten percent of the people in the world fall into this category.

If you're fast-paced and people-oriented, you could be considered an "I" (Influencer). Most sales people are in this category.

If you're people-oriented and methodical, you're in the bottom right category, which is an "S (Steady).

If you're task-oriented and methodical, your personality is a "C" (Cautious and Compliant), shown in the bottom left quadrant. People in the financial and technology worlds are often in this category, as well as scientists.

We're all extreme in one of the four quadrants. No matter what quadrant you're in, though, doesn't make you good or bad; it's just the way you process the world.

Here's the example I share from the stage to explain why you need to understand DISC: If you're in France and you don't speak French, you'll get along fine. If you're in France and you do speak French, you'll get along better. Similarly, if you go through life and you don't know how to speak DISC (communicating with someone according to their personality style), you get along fine. However, if you can speak DISC, you can communicate at a much more impactful level. DISC is similar to a language, and it's quite powerful.

If you want to know more about DISC personality profiling, visit Dr. Rohm's website at personalityinsights.com. One of the interesting things you'll find there is that he has assessment profile tools available for kids as young as four years old. And if you're interested in applying the DISC principles on your way to leadership *Mastery*, you can also visit my website at www.tonyjeary.com to find out more about our Discstyles™ Leadership Report,

Highlights of the Four Basic Styles for Your Study

D—Dominant (Direct)
Key Characteristics:
- Driven by need to be in charge and achieve
- Goal-oriented go-getters
- Focus on no-nonsense approaches to results

How to adapt to Driver/Dominant style:
- Don't waste their time (they're time sensitive)
- Be organized and to the point

- Give bottom-line information with options (in writing)
- Appeal to sense of accomplishment—they're goal-oriented

I—Inspiring (Friendly and Funny)

Key Characteristics:
- Friendly, enthusiastic, like to be with the action
- Thrive on admiration, acknowledgment, and compliments
- Persuasive and warm; build great alliances
- Optimistic and charismatic

How to adapt to Influencer/Interactive Style:
- Give recognition freely
- Support their ideas and opinions
- Be ready to be social with them and get to know them

S—Supportive (Step by Step)

Key Characteristics:
- Warm and nurturing (very people-oriented)
- Relaxed disposition makes them approachable
- Loyal
- Risk-averse

How to adapt to Steady Style:
- Earn their trust and show sincere interest
- Talk feelings, not facts (want approval)
- Never back into a corner

C—Cautious (Every Detail)

Key Characteristics:
- Analytical, persistent, and systematic problem-solvers
- Detail-oriented
- Enjoy perfecting processes and working to results
- High expectations of selves and others (can be critical)

How to adapt to Compliant Style:
- Be sensitive to their time
- Give them data, details
- Be systematic, logical, well-prepared, and exact

BOOK 15
BUILDING YOUR
DREAM HOME

As you know by now, I strongly believe that you get the best results out of life, both personally and professionally, when you're strategic about everything, even when building a home. Have you ever considered that? Strategically planning every detail about your new home—your dream home—so it really aligns with your priorities sets you and your family up for years of over-the-top enjoyment and impact.

Our clients are people who are already successful, and they come to TJI because they want to be even more successful. Many of them are at or near the stage of building their dream home when we take them on as clients. Some have already started. Each family is different, of course. A dream home for some would look totally different than a dream home for others.

I've owned hundreds of homes in a previous business and have built dozens, including my own dream home where my family and I have lived for over twenty years.

I'm now building our second dream home, a penthouse in a high-rise condo a block from our new RESULTS! Center. Through it all, I've learned that the real win is putting strategic effort into connecting with the architect and the builder, along with their subcontractors, so you're more likely to end up with the kind of refinements and the timeline you want.

What does the book say?

I teamed up with my decorator/designer and wrote a book with ten chapters, based on the ten stages of building a new home—from the pre-work and land preparation to the interior detail, floor finish, and final stage (see details in the content graphic below). Each stage lists specific action items for the homeowners to do to facilitate the building process and bring about the best results.

Throughout the book, we encourage great ideas like taking pictures as you see things you like and collecting websites and samples so you'll be ahead of the game in each stage. Then you can communicate those distinctions with the architects as they're drawing your home and with the builder as they're putting it together. We encourage you to plan smartly and know the process so you can be ready for the next step, no matter the size of your home.

How will the book help you?

Building a dream home is hard work, and yet it doesn't have to be drudgery. It can be a joy. The key is to know what you're doing and to be organized and avoid unpleasant surprises. This book will help you plan and build the custom home of your dreams. It's in a binder format that allows you to more effectively work and communicate with your architect, builder, designer, etc.

We've included a whole system on budgeting, which most readers appreciate, as well as tips about building a custom home that many people don't think about. For example, most people put electrical outlets in a standard position in the kitchen, where they're more functional for running their appliances. In the nicer homes, though, homeowners often don't want the electrical outlets in plain sight, so they put them on the side of a cabinet or island, or even underneath. That's just one of the nuances I've picked up with my experience in owning so many homes over the years, and it's those kinds of tips that will add to the value of the book for you.

These are the ten stages of building a home. We take you through each stage in the book and give you ideas and action steps that you may have never considered.

People who are building a dream home obviously have the option of customization, and they should be clear on and decide what they want based on what's most important to them (i.e., appearance, privacy, utility, accessibility etc.)

1. Stage 1 - PREWORK

- Design/Preliminary Planning (See Appendix)
- Budget
- Deed Restrictions Review
- Site Planning
- Architect
- Foundation Engineering
- Permits/Codes

2. Stage 2 - LAND PREPARATION

- Excavation
- Positioning

3. Stage 3 - FOUNDATION

- Foundation

4. Stage 4 - ROUGH-IN

- Framing
- Mechanical
- Plumbing
- Electrical
- Fireplace
- Roofing

5. Stage 5 - DRY WORK

- Insulation
- Sheetrock
- Bricking
- Stucco
- Tape, Bed, and Texture

6. Stage 6 - TRIM

- Doors/Trim
- Cabinets

7. Stage 7 - PAINT

- Paint/Stain

(Continued)

8. Stage 8 – INTERIOR DETAIL

- Electrical and Plumbing Trim Out
- Tile
- Wallpaper
- Countertops
- Interior Hardware

9. Stage 9 - FLOOR FINISH

- Finish Flooring

10. Stage 10 – FINAL

- Driveways
- Sidewalks
- Landscaping

I want to clarify here that this is not a certified architecture-specific book. I'm certainly not an architect. I happen to be a builder. The book is simply a great guideline for how to facilitate discussion among all the team members so you can end up with the home of your dreams.

BOOK 16
TOO MANY EMAILS

Emails are clearly a major part of our personal and professional lives today, and yet many people spend as much as one or two hours a day just managing their emails. Does that sound familiar? My friends George Lowe, Marc Harty (one of the leading e-communications strategists in the country), and Sara Bowling got together to write this little handbook to help our clients—and you—manage your emails instead of letting them manage you.

I was coaching the presidents of Walmart at the time, and they wanted to deal with the issue that their people were not processing emails effectively. Interestingly, by the time we wrote the book in 2003, email ineffectiveness was a global problem, and yet the presidents of Walmart were the first to recognize and strategically address it throughout their company. Most companies fail to set standards and train on the subject. Their inability to think strategically and take action to intentionally address the problem facilitates many wasted hours every day. We teach our clients to create an email culture by developing standards and training all of their employees to implement them; virtually everyone is getting too many emails, and they need to be trained on how to manage them properly.

After the book was written, I licensed the content to Walmart. They paid TJI a monthly fee so they could utilize it on their website and teach it internally to their 2.1 million employees. We eventually licensed it to other companies as well.

We started with eighty-three tips in this book, and we found over the years that people are not able to digest that many distinctions. It's too overwhelming for them. George Lowe and I eventually wrote another book called *We've Got to Start Meeting and Emailing Like This* (to be discussed later in this book), in which we condensed the distinctions down to ten in a format that was more easily digested and accepted into a culture. We've impacted many small and large organizations with this work. Where does your company stand on the issue of email effectiveness?

What does the book say?

Too Many Emails will teach you efficiency techniques and best practices focused on the outcome of achieving true email effectiveness. It offers tips on how to handle incoming email quickly and efficiently and presents the five "Bs" of outgoing email presentation: be brief, be clear, be simple, be prompt, and be careful. Then we dedicate a section to creating an effective email culture, with six solid tips on how to gain buy-in throughout the organization.

How will the book help you?

We endorse with all our clients the importance of having written email standards as a powerful ongoing practice. We've included below the sample email standards checklist from *Too Many Emails*.

STANDARDS CHECKLIST

1.   Share Your Topic
   • Fill the topic line
   • Use descriptive titles
   • Write SOS or Urgent for quick response; use FYI for clarity

2. Be Brief
   - Keep emails to one screen
   - For a quick response, be brief in your request
3. Remember, Style Counts
   - Use bulleted phrases
   - Use numbered lists
   - Use short, separated paragraphs
4. Identify Yourself
   - Use a standard signature that is always attached
   - Include your full name, title, phone number, and other pertinent information
   - Include tag line or motto if applicable—keep it brief
5. Answer Promptly
   - Answer work email on the same day, when possible
   - Answer personal email within one to three days
   - Be consistent with your responses so recipients will know what to expect
   - Use auto-responders if you will be unavailable for a day or longer
6. Be Careful What You Say
   - Don't forget that what you write is permanent
   - Don't respond in anger—save a draft and review later
7. Delete Frequently
   - Keep a clean mailbox
   - Create folders to organize your emails
   - Delete emails you don't need for future reference
8. Manage Your CCs
   - Only use CCs when really needed
   - If you receive CCs, read them and file or delete immediately
9. Say NO to junk mail
   - Don't forward chain letters—they cause stress and aggravation
   - Remember company policies against using company email for personal use
10. Remember the Personal Touch
    - Remember the power of a personal note
    - If best, make a phone call

11. Build an Email Arsenal
   - Save email addresses
   - Email relevant or useful items to others
12. Build an Email Etiquette Culture
   - Influence others to use time-saving techniques when communicating

BOOK 17
WINNING SEMINARS

Are seminars a part of your life? If you're a professional trainer or speaker, in sales and marketing, a non-profit professional, in multi-level marketing, or in any other position that uses the power of seminars and workshops to teach, train, attract business, or just to spread your message, this book is a must-read for you. The concepts we share in this ultimate seminar sourcebook will help you plan and conduct highly effective seminars, workshops, or events that are a "win-win" for both you and your participants.

About twenty years ago I was coaching many of the executives of New York Life, including the chairman. At the time, they had thirty-seven different approved seminars for their agents (10,000 agents in the US alone), and they commissioned me to organize these seminars to make them more accessible. As TJI executed the engagement, we realized it was an excellent opportunity to write a book to help people strategically plan and conduct great seminars and workshops (an *Elegant Solution*).

What does the book say?

The book gives you great tools and resources to help you plan, design, prepare for, and deliver a winning event with less stress and more efficiency, including examples of best practices.

How will the book help you?

Here are ten great takeaways that relate to planning winning events:

1. One of the favorite takeaways has been the teaching on how to get people to attend your seminars. Early and efficient planning often translates into larger audiences, so we've included below a copy of the Seminar Planning Process Map to help you make planning decisions in a timely manner.

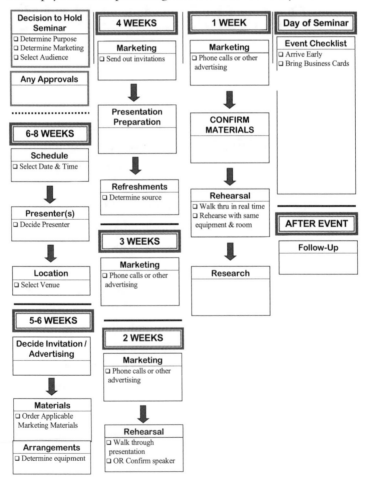

2. Develop a big-picture outline of your seminar content by using the 3-D Outline™ template we provide in Book 1, *Inspire Any Audience*. Start by creating a winning title for your event and identifying your desired outcomes and objectives. Then break your desired outcomes into subtopics, segments, or elements and make an initial time allocation for each item. And finally, identify what (the content), why (tie back to your objectives), and how (method of delivery) for each segment of each module.

3. Here are a few strategies you may want to use to make your content solid and more interesting:
    - Use hands-on demonstrations to help you explain a key learning point. You can even have a participant help you to make it more memorable.
    - Provide documented reports, facts (or even trivia), or statistics that add credibility to your content.
    - Tell interesting stories to help make your content appealing. Find stories that relate to your topic and have a key learning point.
    - Share realistic case studies to merge your point with specific "real-world" experience and make it easier for your participants to shift the information to their own situation.
    - Give relevant examples to help create a mental model that participants can refer to as they assimilate the content you're introducing.
    - Use creative illustrations (pictures, diagrams, photographs, graphics, or visual aids) that exemplify your concept and engage the visual learner.
    - Provide authoritative sources to reinforce and add credibility to your information. Make sure the source is perceived as trustworthy and of higher influence.

4. To energize your audience, keep their attention, and gain their involvement, use a variety of these strategies:
    - Participant workbooks or "note-takers"
    - Open-ended questions
    - Table-team activities

- Brainstorming
- Competitive teams
- Partners
- Role-playing
- Quizzes
- Q&A
- Skits
- Games
- Music
- Activities and exercises
- *Business Entertainment* (an appropriate fun factor)

5. Here's a five-step process for getting your point across:
   1. Introduce the concept
   2. Present and explain the concept or demonstrate the skill
   3. Involve and engage your audience
   4. Get feedback of the applied value/concept
   5. Summarize the concept and call for action

6. Understanding your audience and how adults learn enables you to structure your seminar in a way that will achieve your desired outcomes. First, know *who* your participants are to get a better idea of which learning methodologies you need to incorporate into your presentation. Then know and understand these three sensory modes of learning so you can provide a positive learning experience for all of your participants:
   - Visual (learns by seeing)
   - Auditory (learns by listening)
   - Kinesthetic (learns by hands-on experiences)

7. In your opening few minutes, you'll connect with your audience in either a positive or negative way. What and how you communicate during your opening will quickly determine your audience's perception regarding:
   - Your credibility
   - How much fun they're likely to have
   - How much they are likely to learn
   - How much buy-in you'll receive
   - Their first impressions of how and what to expect during the seminar

8. The do's and don'ts of opening your seminar:

    Do begin:

    - On time
    - With great enthusiasm and energy

    Don't start:

    - Late
    - With an apology
    - Slow and dull
    - Unprepared

9. Here are some great tips for using visual aids:

    - Be sure the visual *supports* what you're communicating rather than *becoming* the message.
    - Visuals should focus on participants' input and contribution as much as possible.
    - Remember to not lose the personal touch. People today want you to connect with them—not just "wow" them.
    - The longer the event, the more effective and important it is to use different kinds of visuals.
    - The more visuals you use, the more likely it is for something to go wrong, so be prepared with a "Plan B" to make sure the show goes on regardless of conditions/failures, without making your audience uncomfortable.
    - Practice with each visual so you are comfortable and can concentrate on the audience rather than the logistics of the visual.
    - For best effectiveness and the least amount of distraction, practice where you're going to stand while using the visuals.
    - Don't speak with your back to the audience while working with the visuals.
    - It's distracting to have information visible that is not being discussed at the time. Wait until talking about that topic to show the visual or bring up the slide. Use

"blind" slides for lists of things so prior points remain visible as you reveal the next one.

10. Your closing leaves the last impression most of your audience members will have of the seminar, so make it a great one. You want your audience to leave on an inspired, energetic note, so make the end of your presentation as enthusiastic, to the point, and benefit-rich as the beginning was. Here are a few tips:

- Review your objectives and tell your audience how each objective was met.
- Review your key concepts to demonstrate a high-level, big-picture view of the ideas you presented. Here you have the opportunity to give maximum punch to your ideas by presenting them in their most concentrated and integrated form.
- Return to the expectations your audience contributed during your opening and show them how you met their expectations. If some weren't met, say, because they were outside the scope of the topic, address that in a positive way.
- Clear out the "parking lot." Address any issues that arose during the event that you left to address at a different time. Sometimes these "parking lot" questions get answered or resolved during the natural course of your presentation. It's essential to deal with these issues decisively, even if that means telling the person who brought it up that you will get more information and get back with them later. (Then make sure you do!)
- Thank your audience for their attention and participation.
- The last thing you do in any seminar or workshop is the final inspiration and call to action that should lead your participants out into the world feeling powerful and capable of implementing your ideas (or purchasing your product). End with an inspirational quote or anecdote that brings it home to everyone. Keep it short, no longer than two to three minutes, and be sure to do your best to connect with your audience on a personal, human level.

BOOK 18
136 EFFECTIVE
PRESENTATION TIPS

At the time this book was written, speaking before a group was number one on the list of greatest personal fears among Americans. (And according to various sources, it's still either number one or number two today.) Is that one of your top fears? If so, you'll love this book!

My friend Dave Cottrell is CEO and president of CornerStone Leadership Institute, one of the nation's largest publishers of management and leadership resources. He and I started publishing together many years ago, and this was one of the first books we co-authored. We wanted to put together a sort of "quick-start" manual that captured my expertise in Presentation Mastery™ to help people be their best when they're invited to make a presentation. It's a great table read—you can sit at your kitchen table and read a few points each day, or you can take an hour or two to read it all the way through.

What does the book say?

Just as the title says, the book gives 136 tips on how to make effective presentations. It's a small handbook that packs a powerful punch, delivering valuable tips that take you all the way from getting started with your presentation (including how to move from nervous to natural) to gaining buy-in with an effective close.

How will the book help you?

We've selected for your review a collection of the most helpful tips that will help you inspire, inform, and influence anyone, anywhere, anytime.

Moving From Nervous to Natural

1. Remember that life is a series of presentations! Both in business and in your personal life, you make dozens of presentations each day.
2. Psyche yourself up. You have something to say that others need to hear, or you would not have been asked to make the presentation.
3. Remember this: Most people in the audience want you to do well. They are on your side.
4. Be yourself. Be "real." Your presentation is really not about being perfect; it's about *connecting with others* and delivering a sincere message.
5. The reason most people get nervous when they're presenting is because they fear the unknown. How will the audience react? How is the room set up? Is the equipment going to work? The more you prepare, the more unknowns become known.

Getting Your Act Together

1. You need to begin with a good foundation. The foundation for any presentation should be clearly defined with written objectives before you develop the agenda. The agenda facilitates the reaching of your objectives.
2. Know your audience. Spend time thinking about your participants' real needs and wants.

3. Complete the 3-D Outline™ (see the template in Book 1, *Inspire Any Audience*) to quickly identify and quantify a lot of information (the what, why, and how) in a small amount of space and time.

4. Greet as many people as you can when they arrive. Smile, introduce yourself, and shake some hands.

Beginning Strong

1. There are three things audience members love: respect of their time, rapport, and entertainment.

2. When you step in front of the room, your smile should confidently suggest, "I'm glad to be here."

3. Within the first few minutes, mention characteristics you have in common with the audience. Acceptance is sometimes built on common experiences.

4. Demonstrate that you are ready, prepared, and credible. Tell them about the time you spent preparing for them; just don't go overboard!

Setting the Tone

1. Prepare the audience. Let them know the three P's: purpose (objectives), process (agenda), and payoff (benefits to them).

2. You're delivering a total message that includes words, visual effects, audio effects, and an intangible aura that will either build or detract from your image as a presenter. Make sure you have properly prepared all of the elements of your message, not just the words.

3. Start on time, stick to the subject, and end on time or renegotiate.

Involve the Audience

1. One of the best ways to keep your audience's attention is to get them involved (facilitation).

2. Ask your audience to write things down.

3. Call your audience members by name. People feel important when you remember their name.

4. To maintain emotion and involvement, answer the audience's number one question, "What is in this presentation for me?" early and often.
5. Use analogies and stories when appropriate.
6. Give your audience a dose of *Business Entertainment* to keep them involved. That could be an activity, a video, or anything that keeps the audience involved and happy.

Maximize Visual Aids

1. PowerPoint presentations should contain limited text. Keep graphics simple and few in number.
2. Flip charts are best used in meetings of less than fifty people. Write big, and use multiple flip charts when appropriate.
3. Organize handouts to match your presentation. Provide plenty of space for notes on your handouts, and always prepare 10 percent more than you think you'll need.

Tips on Gaining Buy-In

1. Tell a story that reinforces your point.
2. Don't fake an answer. Your willingness to research and find the correct answer will often impress the audience more than the willingness to give any answer even if it's an incorrect one.

The Summary and Closing

1. Summarize as you go to prepare the audience intellectually and emotionally for the close.
2. In your closing summary, set the stage by reaffirming value to the audience and preparing them for the emotional punch of the close. A closing call to action reminds the audience that words only matter when they lead to action.
3. Keep your closing short and powerful.

These are just the tip of the iceberg. If you want the advantage of 106 more powerful tips to help you deliver a win for you and your audiences every time you present, we invite you to get this little book. (Visit tonyjeary.com.)

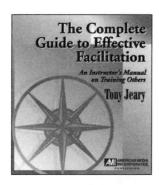

BOOK 19
THE COMPLETE GUIDE TO EFFECTIVE FACILITATION

If you've ever been asked to assist a team in resolving a conflict, lead a work group as it redesigned a process, help a friend plan a party, or interact with a colleague to resolve an issue, you've been a facilitator. Facilitation is a mixture of skill, technique, and strategy. A facilitator is an objective guide who keeps a meeting or a presentation moving in an appropriate direction. Instead of working toward a personal agenda, a facilitator helps a group define and achieve its own goals. The facilitator is also a presenter, and presentation is a skill in itself.

In the past, businesses often hired a consultant to tell them what to do. Now consultants are often more like coaches who strategically facilitate a process that allows team members to figure out what to do. That's what I do every day with my clients. They're some of the brightest people in the world, and they and their teams already know tons. The skill is to draw the best answers from them and then add more. And here's the bonus when facilitation is done correctly: After the participants create the solution, they will be better motivated and will have mental ownership at a higher level in the plan, the actions they decide on, and often the strategy.

By the time I wrote this book and the next one in our series, *Training Other People to Train*, I was beginning to develop a real niche in training. I published both of these books with Todd McDonald, the outstanding publisher for American Media. You may remember that Todd is the one who introduced me to Brian Tracy, who has had an extraordinary influence on my life and hence in many of my published works, including these two books.

What does the book say?

The book is a comprehensive manual on training others that includes such helpful distinctions as understanding the six paradoxes of facilitation and the characteristics of a good facilitator:

Six Paradoxes of Facilitation
1. Think *Planned Spontaneity*. Be prepared, and yet flexible and open to the flow of the group.
2. Fulfill *group* objectives by appealing to participants' *self-interest* ("what's in it for me?").
3. Respect and work with *all* participants, including those who are loud and obnoxious. They will often grow into being worthy of that respect.
4. Balance neutrality and involvement.
5. Teach participants to follow instructions while being creative and thinking for themselves.
6. You can only become a stronger facilitator by acknowledging your weaknesses.
Characteristics of a Good Facilitator
People Skills—Listens well, has a genuine interest in how others think and feel, and is a natural mediator

Objectivity—Helps the group set reasonable goals, respect personal differences, and tolerate unique ideas
Self-Awareness—Has a realistic understanding of personal strengths and weaknesses, which allows for a fair evaluation of motives for accepting/rejecting ideas
Communication Skills—Is a clear communicator who helps others clarify their thoughts and feelings; tunes into body language, unspoken messages, and underlying emotions
Credibility—Perceived as believable and trustworthy because of: • Credentials • Expertise and depth of knowledge • Personal experiences • Level of preparedness • Enthusiasm and openness • Appearance • Language • Level of confidence • Ability to relate

We also include in the appendix many helpful worksheets, checklists, and more.

How will the book help you?

Here's one of the core takeaways from this work: When most people are planning their presentations, they think of the amount of time they will be talking. They often fail to take into account the fact that they're much more impactful when they have involvement from their participants—asking them questions, getting them to write things down, breaking them into subgroups, etc. So to help you master the facilitation balance when you're planning your next presentation, ask yourself this question: *What percentage of the time should I be talking, and what percentage of the time should the audience members be talking?*

We've included below a valuable tool called "Facilitation Dos and Don'ts," which recaps many of the highlights of the book for you.

	Facilitation
	DOS
1	Create an atmosphere for creativity, learning and experimenting, brainstorming, and effective problem-solving.
2	Assist your team in thinking creatively, opening up new opportunities, and tapping into existing knowledge.
3	Work with the group to help them discover their own secrets, give feedback on their progress, and then be a catalyst for change.
4	Keep the group focused on the objectives.
5	Establish objectives and criteria for measuring progress and success.
6	Defuse conflict by redirecting their energies in a constructive manner.
7	Clarify to the group their benefit for participating (what's in it for them).
8	Provide pragmatic learning through hands-on exercises and involvement.
9	Meet as many participants as possible before you begin in order to connect.
10	Use buzzwords/terms everyone is familiar with.
11	Leverage participant's names.
12	Plan and use breaks to meet and connect with the participants.
13	Be an active listener and seriously consider any concerns or complaints.
14	Mirror the speech patterns and speaking speed of your audience.
15	Realistically assess the personal strengths and weaknesses of the participants and be willing to be open to someone's suggestion that is different from your own.
16	Establish credibility by being believable and trustworthy. Use credentials and personal experiences and be fully prepared and confident.

(Continued)

	Facilitation
17	Get people involved by asking them to write things down, answer questions, break into groups, create competitive teams, or prepare team reports.
18	Show respect for participants' time, comfort, and intelligence by having the appropriate materials ready, having the room set properly, and starting on time.
	DON'TS
19	Don't make jokes or inappropriate comments about participants.
20	Don't present all in one mode. Favor different sensory modes for better learning (visual, auditory, kinesthetic, etc.).
21	Don't look above the crowd. Make eye contact with individuals.
22	Don't be timid. Communicate clearly and present ideas assertively.
23	Don't be too rigid with your timing. Keep your promises about time, and yet remember that in a facilitation session, getting to the issues involved is a key consideration.

BOOK 20
TRAINING OTHER
PEOPLE TO TRAIN

With the rapid pace of change in business and technology today, people need to continually learn new and different things, and companies obviously need to provide ongoing training. Really, whether you're a supervisor, manager, group leader, team leader, mentor, or you hold any other position where you work with a team, you need to be strategic about training other people in the organization. Today, much of the training is done through videos, webinars, and other electronic media.

Training the trainer (also called "T-3") was one of my specialties when I built my large training organization in the nineties and was training people around the world. I refined my skills to the point that I was regarded and hired as a world expert, which supported my Mr. Presentation™ brand. (As a side note, the record number of T-3 programs I led in one week was eleven. That was almost an impossible feat, because it required that in one week's time I study and understand the content of eleven programs, often in different languages, to the point that I was able to train the trainers in each one.

What does the book say?

The work has eight powerful modules that teach you things like:

- The different ways people learn (adult learning, sensory learning modes, and the four stages of learning)
- How to handle the "people side" of training (meeting your audience's expectations, handling difficult people, and questioning and listening skills)
- How to create a training session (determining your outcomes and objectives through the five-step funneling process and incorporating valuable training methods and materials)
- The importance of the opening (the first three minutes) and the overview (your objectives and agenda)
- How to conduct the training (great guidelines on presenting, conducting exercises, and facilitating, as well as how to motivate your audience with energizers and *Business Entertainment*™)

How will the book help you?

One of the most valuable takeaways from this book is understanding the importance of using tools to achieve consistency in your message when you're cascading it down, whether that's through training or just passing on information throughout your organization. For example, this morning I recorded a video for one of our clients. We recently completed a company passport for them (a small booklet the size of a passport) that sets out their strategy for 2018. The video will accompany the passport when it's sent out to their thirty-one dealerships to ensure that all dealership personnel are receiving the same message. So as I was recording the video, I was training all of their managers at the same time and in the same way on how to train their people to implement their strategy for 2018. The consistency you can achieve with tools is invaluable in cascading your message.

BOOK 21
COMMUNICATION MASTERY
NLP MADE SIMPLE
AND
BOOK 22
UNDERSTANDING NLP FOR
PRESENTATION MASTERY

NLP stands for Neuro-Linguistic Programming. "Neuro" refers to the study of the brain and nervous system, and "Linguistic" refers to language and its characteristics. Programming is the development and implementation of a strategy or plan. So Neuro-Linguistic Programming is a long-winded way of describing the study and use of language as it affects our brain and therefore our behavior. To put it more simply, it's a study of how we speak on the unconscious level.

I have been continually fascinated with Neuro-Linguistic Programming since 1986. After I wrote the first book, *Communication Mastery: NLP Made Simple*, I was invited by a publisher to team up with some other NLP experts to put together an assessment tool. So my second book on the subject, *Understanding NLP for Presentation Mastery*, is a spin-off of the first one.

I look at NLP as a language in and of itself, much like DISC, because observing how other people unconsciously speak and responding to them in the same way is as effective as speaking in a common language.

You may remember the analogy I gave in Book 14 *Presenting with Style* about speaking the DISC "language." Going through life knowing how to speak both DISC (communicating with someone according to their personality style) and NLP (communicating on the unconscious level) gives as powerful an advantage as, say, going to France knowing how to speak French. If you can speak DISC and NLP, you can communicate at a high level. In essence, they are languages that anyone can speak if you want to take the time to learn them. As a matter of fact, I taught both DISC and NLP to my kids as they were growing up, rather than investing the time and effort to teach them a foreign language, because I wanted them to have that advantage every day of their lives. How about you?

What do the books say?

The book is primarily about strategically taking control of your communication. Before you can *really* communicate with another person, you must be intentional about respecting his or her unique point of view of the world. It doesn't matter what you *meant* to communicate; all that really matters is the other person's response to what they understood. It's a matter of increasing your awareness, skill sets, and techniques to more strategically and effectively influence people to action.

When you employ these NLP skills, you can enhance your ability to deal with roadblocks and/or issues that slow down the process of closing business so you can *shorten* sales cycles and *increase* your effectiveness.

How will the books help you?

Here are twelve skills associated with NLP that will enhance your ability to communicate with your audience or prospect:

1. Modeling:

   <u>What it is</u>: The study of what works well and then duplicating accordingly for similar results.

   <u>Why to use it</u>: Accelerate your success by using proven methods, thoughts, and behaviors.

   <u>How to use it</u>: Benchmark people, processes, and even tangibles (such as websites, closing scripts, and physiology).

2. Rapport:

   <u>What it is</u>: Relationship, especially one of mutual trust or affinity. Rapport comes from commonality. The ways we get commonality are dress, matching and mirroring, posture, mannerisms, and even pace (the way we communicate).

   <u>Why to use it</u>: People are influenced by people they trust. Trust often comes from rapport, and rapport comes from commonalities.

   <u>How to use it</u>: Search for commonalities through upfront research as well as through various communication opportunities with the audience or individual audience members.

3. Pacing and Leading:

   <u>What it is</u>: Gaining alignment with the rhythm of your audience and then leading them toward your agenda.

   <u>Why to use it</u>: When you match a person's pace, they feel connected, both consciously and unconsciously.

   <u>How to use it</u>: Create a rhythm that gets people into a pattern, and often you can drive them in the direction you desire.

   Example: Getting people to respond to your requests during your talk, such as raising their hands or talking to others.

4. Word Choice:

   <u>What it is</u>: People have preferences for the way they represent things in their mind. It's usually a preference of one of three senses:

- Seeing (I see ... It appears to me ...)
- Hearing (I hear you ... That sounds like ...)
- Feeling (Pain in the neck ... Get in touch with ...)

<u>Why to use it</u>: People like to use information in their own style.

<u>How to use it</u>: Identify the sensory mode your audience prefers, and adjust to that mode of communication.

VIP (Very Important Point): Use sensory-related words that your audience/prospect prefers. If in a group setting, use all three, both verbally and in your slides and handouts.

Visual	Auditory	Kinesthetic
Look at	Sounds good	I feel your pain
Get the picture	It says	Does that make sense
Do you see it	Industry says	Exciting
Show me	Echo	How do you feel
Image	Do you hear me	Understand
Point of view		
Observe		
Focus in		

5. Embedded Commands:

    <u>What it is</u>: Phrases are often embedded within a sentence that can have an unconscious impact on the action that people take. Example: "Please remember what I'm saying. Take a lot of great notes." (The first phrase is the real result you want. Taking notes is the feature, or the hard action. Remembering is the ultimate goal you want.) Another example: "We need to finish this book now so we can move on." (The word "now" is a subtle indication of the speed with which you need to execute.)

    <u>Why to use it</u>: It's an easy way to step people further toward your cause or action.

    <u>How to use it</u>: Place phrases within communication that lead people to the desired action you want them to take.

VIP: Ensure your word choices support the action you want
to happen.

6. Anchors/Conditioned Responses:
    <u>What it is</u>: We respond unconsciously based on stimulus
    response; anchors are triggers that stimulate our responses,
    both mentally and emotionally. People have built-in responses
    to certain stimuli; it can come from all senses.
    (Pavlov's theory of the dogs salivating is a great way to
    understand this concept.)
    <u>Why to use it</u>: Choosing words that stimulate positive anchors
    in people's minds can help you move them to the desired
    state of mind and the action you want them to take (and the
    opposite can also happen with a negative anchor; these need to
    be avoided).
    Positive Word Association:
    >   Use agreement vs. contract
    >   Use partner vs. customer or client
    >   Use value
    >   Use challenge or opportunity vs. problem
    >   Use upgrade
    >   Use cost-effective
    >   Use return, profitability, margin, effectiveness, etc.

    <u>How to use it</u>: Fire off responses based on anchors already
    set and transfer that state of mind to your offer. Create the
    response to a particular stimuli.
    VIP: In your communication, be aware that the words you
    use can trigger mental and emotional responses in your
    audience.

7. Future Pacing:
    <u>What it is</u>: Verbalizing a potential future reality way in
    advance of just a few steps. A future pace is allowing the
    person to already see the benefits of the potential of utilizing
    your product or service. So taking the steps to demonstrate it
    is a much easier yes.
    <u>Why to use it</u>: It is a relatively easy way to get people to take
    the first steps and gain momentum toward your cause.

How to use it: Communicate way beyond the first steps what you want to have happen (like in a sale). Example: Often, I'll use a combination of embedded commands and future pacing when I say, "So at the end of the day when we've gone through these objectives, we will have had a very productive session, and we will have included a few extras so we ensure we have exceeded your expectations."

8. Pattern Interrupts:

What it is: Often when selling someone on your point of view (or product/service), they will get off track and focused on something else. Pattern interrupts will help focus them on your desired message.

Why to use it: Being able to shock them into a new direction of thinking can often lead you to the buy-in you desire.

How to use it: You can do it by use of body language (abruptly standing up or moving into the crowd) or tone (tactfully raising your voice). These are the two common ways that work in a sales-type scenario.

VIP: Tactfully utilize the "shock factor" to interrupt a person or group's pattern of thinking and to position yourself to reguide their thoughts.

9. Reframing:

What it is: People often get stuck in a certain frame of reference. Sometimes it's due to a limited understanding; sometimes it's simply by focused choice.

Why to use it: Giving an audience member (one or many) a different way or a different frame of reference of thinking about a certain subject can often move that person's thinking to where you want it to be.

How to use it: Recognize that people often come to a decision based on their frame of reference. Be aware and prepared to give them a different way of thinking.

10. Looping:

What it is: Looping is telling a story within a story that causes the audience members' attention to be focused on you and what you are saying.

Why to use it: If you want to keep a person's attention, you can create a certain thinking that causes curiosity for you to continue.

> **Note**: If you begin telling a story and you shift in the middle of a story to another line of thinking, you can often semi-control a person's attention.

How to use it: At the beginning of an influential presentation, set up things that cause curiosity so you keep people wanting to hear what you have to say. Example: I will use documents or processes and I'll move to another document/process before I complete the first one.

11. Confusion:

What it is: A state of mind that people fall into or can be put into; a state that people do not want to stay in.

Why to use it: All people want to escape a state of confusion, and they will strive to quickly move out of confusion, even if it seems partially logical.

How to use it: You can create confusion or catch people in confusion and then tactfully give them a solution that they'll move forward to escape this emotional state. Example: "So here is what you need to do…"

12. Chunking:

What it is: Managing the level of detail that is the most effective to move people to your way of understanding.

Why you use it: Sometimes you'll want to "chunk up," focusing the discussion on less of the details and give more of the big picture.

> **Note**: Sometimes—especially when personalities that are detail-oriented are involved—chunking down is the best way for people to receive your message.

How to use it: Chunk to the level that is most appropriate to accomplish your objective, based on the way people want to receive it (their style)—50,000 feet, 10,000 feet, or 500 feet.

Invest some time in studying NLP, and you'll see a whole new world open up to you. The ability to speak a universal language could present endless possibilities for better results in both your personal and business lives.

BOOK 23
10 ESSENTIALS FOR DRIVING EXECUTION

Execution is one of my three foundational words (to get the results you want, you have to take constant action and build momentum). It drives home the heart of what I teach every day to top achievers all over the world. We published this little book several years before we published my signature book *Strategic Acceleration* about the methodology of *Clarity, Focus, and Execution.* However, I had been pulling together and teaching distinctions on execution for years, so I took ten of those concepts and crafted this little book.

Clarity, focus, and execution are all equally important. Clarity and focus provide the roadmap for execution. However, I think you would probably agree with me that *nothing happens without execution.* Right?

I wrote *10 Essentials for Driving Execution* as a favor for one of the top three executives for Walmart. At the time, I was coaching all the top executives at Walmart, including the president and the chairman, and they were really drilling down on execution with the almost two million people working for them.

What does the book say?

The book is basically a list of ten major essentials for strategically driving execution in any organization, with distinctions for each of the ten essentials.

Execution is action at all levels: good, great, and *Mastery*. Good execution is getting things done; great execution is getting things done fast and on purpose; and *Mastery* execution is about getting the right things done (actions that have been intentionally and strategically thought out), and getting them done fast and on purpose. You can create the greatest plan in the world and establish the most focused goals imaginable; yet if you fail to execute, you're not going to achieve them. It's that simple. The powerful thing about it is, the world flocks to people who get it done! Are you one of those people? I have devoted my life to helping high-achieving leaders execute to get the right results faster!

How will the book help you?

If you put these ten essentials to work, you'll find that you're more intentionally strategic about getting things done and getting better results.

10 Essentials for Driving Execution

1. Plan and Communicate Your Vision
   - Determine and write clear objectives.
   - Define and document supporting actions.
   - Internally test your plan with a focus group.
   - Identify your communication channels.
   - Manage and integrate all communication channels appropriately.
   - Maintain and reinforce message consistency.

2. Set Clear Goals and Expectations
    - Develop goals that align with each other.
    - Facilitate team buy-in.
    - Communicate true expectations.
    - Fully define and communicate the "why."
    - Cascade clear role definitions through all levels and functional areas.
3. Prioritize Hourly
    - Periodically audit your prioritization skills.
    - Leverage lists.
    - Reassess and prioritize your lists hourly, daily, and weekly (on your phone, tablets, computer, or whatever method compliments your personal style).
4. Conduct Effective Meetings and Presentations
    - Leverage the *Meeting MAGIC* model (below).
    - Utilize the CPA (Content/Presentation/Audience) Presentation Model (below).
    - Understand and use the 3-D Outline™ process that defines the primary dimension of "What" is involved, the secondary dimension of "Why", and the third dimension, "How" (see below).

Meeting Magic
- Decide to meet or not to meet.
- Utilize a good agenda.
- Set good guidelines.
- Create involvement.
- Execute with clear actions.

CPA Presentation Model
- Content
    - Preparation:
        - Gather intelligence
        - Survey audience
        - Pre-assignment
        - Meet just before
        - Host introduction

- **P**resentation
  - Opening
  - Body
  - Closing
- **A**udience
  - Follow-Up:
    - Electronic handout
    - Meet just after
    - Email
    - Telephone
    - Mail

The 3-D Outline™ - The Ultimate Presentation Tool! (See template in Book 1: *Inspire Any Audience*)

- Title your meeting for easier retrieval.
- Have three written objectives that begin with an action word (such as convey, share, brainstorm, motivate).
- Define the designated time and use the column to break down each of the "What's."
- Chunk the meeting outline into an opening, a closing, and primary topics in the "What" column.
- Include one or two words in the "Why" column that describe the value or reason for the "What."
- Vary the delivery, populating the "How" column.

5. Seek Production Before Perfection (PBP)
    - Understand that everyone procrastinates.
    - Procrastination is caused by inefficient thinking.
    - Some examples of inefficient thinking: "It has to be perfect," "The timing has to be right," "I have to have all of the facts," and "I have to have all of the right people before I can get going."
    - PBP says: Get the task or action in motion, and momentum will be on your side.

- Appreciate the concept of *Parallel Progress*—having multiple people doing multiple tasks, not one after another, but at the same time.

6. Delegate to Expand Your Capacity
   - Periodically audit your delegation effectiveness.
   - Manage your lists.
   - Develop, implement, and manage your personal set of delegation performance standards.
   - Communicate clear expectations.
   - Have delegates report back to you on the progress (to have the ball in their court) and give you status on progress, road blocks, and completion.

7. Create Mental Ownership
   - Create a culture of real buy-in.
   - Instill a sense of pride of ownership in your team.
   - Immerse yourself in execution and key details; people emulate their leaders.

8. Manage Change
   - "Change happens so frequently today that one change isn't complete before another is being launched." — William Bridges, *Managing Transitions*
   - In most cases, it isn't the changes themselves that the people resist.
   - Show the picture to people as soon as the change is announced.
   - Clarify your mission. Stability through change demands clarity about what you are trying to do.

9. Handle Setbacks
   - Effectively handling setbacks begins with becoming a "change champion."
   - People deal more easily with change. . .
      - When they know the "why," so provide the "because"
      - When they know how it relates to the execution of the big picture
      - If they know how it personally affects them

10. Provide Gratitude and Praise (Recognition)
- Roll up your sleeves and help your team. A great leader should be dynamically involved.
- A great executor inspires—not crushes—his team.
- Recognize the little things ... not just the big things.
- Challenge your team to catch someone doing something right.
- Encourage praise for people who take action.

BOOK 24
ONE-TO-ONE
PRESENTATIONS

A one-to-one (1.2.1) presentation is probably the most frequently utilized form of communication we have. Think about it: How many times *today* have you interacted with just one other person? Properly handled, an effective one-to-one presentation could help you be a better leader, increase your execution effectiveness, turn conflict into construction, and even influence your customers. This book is intended to help you understand the potential impact of a strategically managed one-to-one presentation and show you ways in which you can improve your existing skill set.

My friend and colleague Greg Kaiser, who was instrumental in helping Ken Blanchard grow his brand, is a brilliant thinker. We became respected colleagues; then he became my intellectual property partner for a while, and he helped me think through many great ideas. In fact, he gave me the idea for the good/great/*Mastery* impact model I use so often today.

One of the things we often talked about is that most presentations are made one-to-one, so we developed this little book together to share our thinking and best practices related specifically to those types of presentations.

What does the book say?

The concept is that one-to-one presentations are where the rubber meets the road in organizations, with respect to ongoing business performance. They're often the place where good ideas catch on, leadership emerges, and peers influence peers toward goals. In fact, one-to-one communications are largely responsible for the success of a business. The degree to which ideas and messages are able to flow through the organization determines how fast an organization can execute corporate strategies and integrate frontline discoveries.

One-to-one presentations flow three directions: top-down, bottom-up, and peer-to-peer. Presentations made in any of these three directions have the potential to radically impact the degree of success your business experiences.

In the book we share the best practices for one-to-one presentations as they apply to interviewing, performance planning, coaching, praise, redirection, and promotions, as well as some powerful ways to help you capitalize on them.

How will this book help you?

Use these two simple tools—the Presentation Mastery™ journey and the Presentation Utilization Chart—to help you strategically manage your one-to-one communications for better results.

After committing to its general disciplines, there are five recurring steps on the Presentation Mastery™ journey:
1. Define your Presentation Universe (see the Presentation Utilization Chart below)
2. Learn and apply Presentation Mastery™ practices and techniques:
    a. Elevated preparedness
    b. Professional delivery
    c. Strategic follow-up
4. Evaluate your presentation effectiveness
5. Incorporate feedback
6. Redefine your goals to increase your impact

Presentation Utilization Chart			
Type of Presentation	Communication	Group Size	Best Uses
1:1	2-way	1	Informational Goal-setting Coaching Re-directing Problem-solving Feedback + or − Evaluation
Small Group (i.e., 10-Minute Daily Meetings, huddles)	1-way 2-way multi-direction group discussion	2-30	Training Skill development Feedback Direction setting Consensus Decision-making
Large Group	1-way	30 +	Awareness Announcement Information-sharing Launch Roll-out
Voicemail/Email	1-way	1	Awareness Announcement Information sharing
Conference/Web Call	1-way 2-way multi-direction group discussion	Many	Training Skill development Feedback Direction setting Consensus Decision-making
Community/Media	1-way	30+	Awareness Announcement Information-sharing

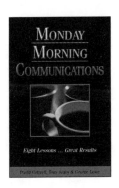

Eight Lessons ... Great Results

David Cottrell, Tony Jeary & George Lowe

BOOK 25
MONDAY MORNING
COMMUNICATIONS

How do you think your team would rate your communication skills on a team survey? Are your emails clear and concise? Are you and your colleagues sending mixed messages? How about your meetings and conference calls? Are they effective?

If there's a chance your ratings might be anything less than stellar, you may relate to Jeni and Michael, the protagonists in my first-ever (and only) fiction book, *Monday Morning Communications*. Jeni and Michael are shocked to discover their communications ratings are so poor. They had not even realized their communications were an issue. How can they step up their game?

My friend and publisher David Cottrell, who has published several books for me under his imprint over the years, wrote a bestselling book called *Monday Morning Leadership*. Since his book had done so well, he and I decided to team up with my friend George

Lowe and create a companion book that was based on my subject of expertise, Presentation Mastery™.

What does the book say?

Monday Morning Communications describes the mentoring that takes place every Monday morning for eight weeks between Tony Pearce, a semi-retired successful business leader, and Jeni and Michael, the two managers who find themselves behind the eight-ball in their communication skills.

How will the book help you?

The charts below summarize many of the main points discussed in the mentoring sessions. Whether you apply them to just your own communications or are in a position to improve the communication culture of your entire organization, we believe you'll see a major impact on your results if you'll be intentionally strategic about putting these powerful distinctions to work.

Communications That Count . . .
. . . have clear objectives. They are designed to cause action, to convey key information and/or to change or reinforce others' thinking.
Our Goals:
1. More communications that go out right enough the first time 2. Better effectiveness and productivity 3. Reduced overall message volume, workload, and stress
You Touch It, You Own It
Senders are *primarily* responsible for the effectiveness of communications. **Receivers** are responsible for identifying problems—it is **not** okay to ignore items you don't understand. **Management** is responsible for systemic issues and availability of common information.

Guidelines

Effective *Communications That Count:*

- have an evident business purpose and specific objectives
- are clear, concise, and direct
- use the most effective and efficient medium for delivery
- include the appropriate people
- use a courteous, positive, businesslike tone
- are complete, correct, and fully thought-through
- provide clear motivation for action for all involved

The Reporter's Questions are your friends. Does your communication have answers to the "who, what when, why, how, where, and how much" questions?

Communications That Count
Media Selection Do's

- Do use face-to-face contacts for sensitive, emotional, or personal topics.
- Do use meetings when collaboration and diverse views are important to generate better solutions and plans.
- Do use email for straightforward, fact-based matters—it can save a lot of time vs. phone calls or meetings.
- Do use the intranet portal to post reports and information, and keep your postings up to date.
- Do use the telephone for matters that require a high degree of interaction. One short call often can do the job of six emails.

Go Slow To Go Fast

Communications That Count
Media Selection Don'ts

- Don't put anything in an email or on the intranet that you wouldn't like to see published on the front page of the newspaper.
- Don't use meetings for matters that can be best handled by individuals (group writing, for example, is very wasteful).
- Don't overuse instant messaging—each one you send is an immediate interruption to the receiver.
- Don't depend on the intranet portal to communicate urgent matters. People need to be alerted by phone or email if something is hot.
- Don't use telephone calls for discussions that require visual references without sending graphics or data via email in advance.

And we'll leave you with the final words of wisdom that Tony Pearce gave to his two protégées:

> Today is your day. You're off to Great Places! You're off and away! You have brains in your head. You have feet in your shoes. You can steer yourself any direction you choose. You're on your own. And you know what you know. And YOU are the one who'll decide where to go.

—Dr. Seuss, *Oh, the Places You'll Go*

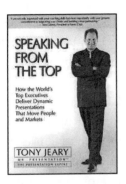

BOOK 26
SPEAKING FROM THE TOP

If you're a CEO or other top executive, you know that your speeches and presentations impact the culture of the organization and the lives and livelihoods of many people. Your words must be carefully crafted and presented in the most favorable environments possible. The messages of top leaders to shareholders, boards of directors, employees, and the general public shape the future of their businesses, and those messages deserve the best treatment.

And yet many CEOs and top leaders overlook the importance of strategically assimilating their teams to help them deliver dynamic presentations that move people and markets.

Since many of our clients are CEOs and corporate presidents, I wanted to craft a book that would help CEOs be more strategic in preparing their presentations, which includes leveraging their teams. In fact, executive assistants and other team members could read the book to discover how to help their leaders even more.

I was very fortunate to have endorsements from the president of Sam's and the president of Ford, two top leaders I've had the privilege of coaching, for the cover of this book.

What does the book say?

The spoken message of an executive reflects the heart and soul of an organization. No speech or executive presentation is as important as the one that comes "from the top." We live in a visual, fast-paced, streamlined world, and the most successful presentations use many dynamic tools to present concepts in concise, powerful, and readily understood ways. This book is written to help corporate leaders expand their thinking and use those tools to the best advantage. Tools give us leverage.

CEOs and other top executives can more easily reach their potential as excellent speakers and presenters when they use the many resources available to them. *Every* word must count, and *every* presentation must be thoroughly prepared and powerfully delivered. When it comes to speechmaking and executive presentations, most leaders need to learn how to better leverage their team's support as they create their speeches.

How will the book help you?

Using the team approach elevates the quality of a presentation. When executives deliver speeches or presentations of any kind, they are delivering total messages that include words, visual effects, audio effects, and an intangible aura that will either build up or detract from their images as leaders. *The key is to bring in the right people for the presentation team at the right time for the right assignments for the right duration*, being sure that each role is filled by a person who has the necessary expertise, background, and desire to help.

A CEO's typical presentation development team should include:
1. Team coordinator
2. Graphics and multimedia coordinator
3. Content specialist (gatherer)
4. Speechwriter/presentation creator
5. Presentation coach

As a senior executive or owner, you have the power and authority to dramatically impact the future of your organization and the personal and professional lives of all who are in the sphere of your influence. People listen to you with an ear for action. They expect you to present an outstanding speech that hits the mark. Take charge. And remember the most important takeaway from this book—strategically put together a team to help you make the most of every presentation opportunity you face, from the preparation all the way through to delivery and follow up.

BOOK 27
NERVOUS TO NATURAL

For many years, I carried the moniker Mr. Presentation™ and traveled the world teaching thousands of people, included top executives from the world's most successful companies, how to present well. Then and even now, since I've moved directly into the realm of helping CEOs and top leaders learn how to better strategize and hence get the right results they're after faster, one of the areas people most frequently ask for help on is the anxiety they feel before they make a presentation. Is that a big concern for you as well?

You want to present well, and a big deterrent to impacting audiences is an obvious lack of confidence, which stems from nervousness. As I mentioned in the narrative for Book 18, *136 Effective Presentation Tips*, speaking before a group is very high on the list of the top fears. If you're in that group, you're not alone! As far as I know, stage fright has never killed anyone; however, people sometimes say they would rather die than give a speech!

What does the book say?

Most people are nervous when it comes to presenting to larger groups for the simple reason that they fear the *unknown*. They don't know how their audience is going to react, for example, or whether they'll forget something. So how do you move the unknown to the known? It's simple—know more.

The more you prepare, the more you know, and the more you know, the more you reduce nervousness. If you rehearse right, you'll know a lot more about your presentation function and content, and your confidence will grow. When you test your equipment and room setup, you'll be more assured of the reliability of the equipment and the ability of your audience to see and hear your presentation. When you research your audience's reactions and feelings about your subject, you'll know you're meeting your audience's needs and hence your objections.

How will the book help you?

We've identified six steps, along with specific actions, for strategically moving from nervous to natural:

1. Preparation
    a. Define your objectives
    b. Know your audience
    c. Study you message/know your content
    d. Use the 3-D Outline™ (see Book 1, *Inspire Any Audience*)
    e. Prepare a checklist
    f. Create a back-up plan
2. Rehearsal
    a. Mental walk-through
    b. Fast walk-through
    c. Full dress rehearsal
3. Setup
    a. The night before: Take it easy and create a relaxed atmosphere for yourself.

b. The day of the presentation: Organize your day so it won't be hectic.

c. Own the presentation environment: Know your room, walk it before the presentation, and make the room mentally yours.

d. Set up and test the equipment: Check everything from lighting to projection, screens, and sound. Do not trust others telling you it works fine. You or your team need to see it firsthand.

e. Establish champions in the audience: Meet and greet the audience so you have a clear beginning for eye contact later on.

f. Isometrics, etc.:

- Press your fingertips gently together; then press harder and hold for a few seconds. You can do this even as you begin speaking (in some cases). No one will know that you're burning bottled stress and reducing nervousness.

- Pull up on the bottom of your chair for five seconds; repeat often.

- Press your palms together tightly; hold and repeat.

- While sitting, let your arms dangle at your sides. Gently rotate your wrists and let your fingers shake loosely. Gently shake the stress out of your fingers, hands, and arms.

- Take several deep, slow breaths.

g. Stretch

h. The last few minutes before "show time": Review your checklist. Be sure everything is done, and your confidence will be strong. Look for current things you can mention when you can present. Visualize yourself giving an amazing presentation.

4. Start Right

a. Your first words: Let your audience know how happy you are to be there.

    b.   Prove you're ready, prepared, and credible: Tell the audience, if possible, about all the prep you've done for them.

    c.   Getting involvement: Get them involved immediately.

5. Keep the Pace

    a.   Set the tone of your presentation: Take it slow and easy, speaking as you do in casual conversation.

    b.   Get audience feedback: Ask for it verbally and watch for it nonverbally; encourage them to ask questions, as well.

    c.   Use activities for audience involvement throughout: music, games, stories, activities, skits, giveaways, etc.

    d.   Pre-summarize: Throughout the presentation pre-summarize to be sure you're covering all the points.

6. The Close

    a.   Have a clear picture of your close before you start your presentation.

    b.   Summarize to review your main points and end confidentially

Expanded Thinking

Since originally publishing this work, we've added two more distinctions that will help you move from nervous to natural:

1. Be real. People care more about your being real than they do about your being perfect.

2. Strategically build *Breathing Spaces* into your presentation. (You create a *Breathing Space* for yourself when you direct your audience's attention away from you with things like showing a video, asking them to write something down, etc.)

Follow these steps, and you'll be delivering with more ease in front of an audience in no time.

BOOK 28
IMAGES OF BEAUTY

My youngest daughter Paige has been captivating people of all ages with her photography since a young age. Many are often in awe of her special eye for angles. She is a talented young lady who loves to serve, encourage others, and bring beautiful moments together to be remembered.

Today, her photography brightens rooms, office spaces, and people's faces all around the globe. (See paigejearyphotogprahy.org and consider contracting her for your next photography project.) Brooke, our oldest, is an exceptional graphic artist. (See her website for the services she offers at www.brookehawkins.myportfolio.com.)

The year Paige was sixteen, I wanted to reverse the norm of Father's Day and give *her* a gift that showed my appreciation for the special daughter she is, versus expecting a gift from her. The greatest gifts I get from my kids are their personal notes and videos affirming our close relationship. As a parent, it's such a blessing to read and experience the love your kids give back to you for what you've poured into their lives. I'm constantly thinking about how I can best live up to being the president of my kids' fan club. (Perhaps that's something you might want to do as well.) So that year I decided to make something special for Paige for Father's Day.

I selected some of the best photographers in the world and researched to see how they created their photography books. Then, using those books as a model, I created a book for Paige with fifty of the best photographs she had taken at that time. I divided the pictures into seven themes, and I named each picture.

What does the book say?
The fifty photographs are arranged into these seven themes: sky, nature, objects, water, people, fun, and sister (her older sister Brooke).

How will the book help you?
For your enjoyment, we have included one picture from each of the seven themes.

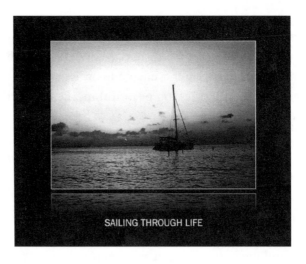

Figure 1: SKY

Figure 2: Nature

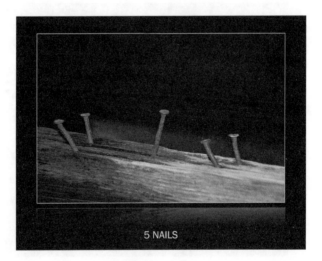

Figure 3: Objects

Figure 4: Water

Figure 5: People

PAIGE IN SAND

Figure 6: Fun

BLONDE ON CARPET

Figure 7: Sister

BOOK 29
PRESENTATION MASTERY
FOR REALTORS

Jim and Linda McKissack started in the real estate business $600,000 in debt, and by the time we authored this book together, they had built their agency's annual sales to $60 million. How did they make that phenomenal transformation? By building their brand through Presentation Mastery™. This book is about using those same Presentation Mastery™ principles to help you build your own brand, present your best self, and increase your income exponentially.

When my oldest daughter Brooke was in second grade, I came to the attention of a very wonderful couple who had a son in the same school and same grade as Brooke. (I remember it like it was yesterday.) In a nutshell, Jim and Linda were a super-high-achieving husband-and-wife real-estate team; in fact, they were the highest-earning profit-sharing members of all 180,000 Keller Williams agents. Even though they were already top achievers, they basically said to me, "We want the best coach, so we want to hire you to grow our thinking." We became very close, and today they are among our very best friends.

Jim and Linda are owners of the McKissack Realty Group, a Keller Williams franchise agency. (They've since turned the operation of their agency over to family members, and Linda has gone on to become one of the top real-estate and entrepreneurial trainers in the world, helping people create leverage and passive income.) When I started coaching them, I helped Jim and Linda realize that in the process of building their business over the years, they had become master presenters. After all, they had made successful presentations on a daily basis for years! That "ah-ha" moment led to our decision to co-author a book to help people expedite their success in real estate by applying both my Presentation Mastery™ methodology and their expertise as exceptional realtors.

What does the book say?

Drawing on our combined wisdom and expertise, the book helps real estate agents to:

- Transform their thinking about building their own brand, hence ...
- Increase their market share in their local real-estate market
- Develop a unique marketing approach that will set them apart from their competitors
- Think differently and change outdated paradigms (which is what I do pretty much every day of my life)

How will the book help you?

Whether you're in real estate or any other industry, you can learn from the powerful distinctions in this book that teach you how to present to build your brand, including these twelve secrets:

1. Learn from and model others.
2. Present yourself as successful—both in actions and appearance.
3. Choose a name with room to grow.
4. Communicate your brand in everything you do, and be consistent.
5. Be bold and different.

6. Tactfully drip or touch people often so they remember you.

7. Choose a motto or a theme to use in your marketing.

8. Leverage your photo(s).

9. Reinforce your brand with good service and added value.

10. Present that you are successful at the specific things your clients want to accomplish.

11. Consistently utilize third-party testimonials.

12. Present your brand to appeal to the different behavioral styles (see Book 14, *Presenting with Style*).

The wealth-building secrets in this book can help you change your thinking and literally transform your life.

BOOK 30
PRESENTING LEARNING

One thing most people in the field of workplace learning and performance haven't learned how to do is persuasively, aggressively, and strategically present the case for learning in language that CEOs understand, embrace, and feel compelled to act upon. If that's your frustration, this book is for you, as it explains and illustrates specific strategies for accomplishing this crucial objective.

I co-authored this book with Tony Bingham, the president of the largest training organization in the world. Formerly called the American Society for Training and Development (ASTD), it's now the Association for Talent Development (ATD), and it's 55,000 members strong. Their members come from more than 120 countries and work in public and private organizations in every industry sector. This excellent organization helps learning professionals build their business acumen, understand the profession's role in addressing skills gaps, and connect their work to the strategic priorities and key measures of business leaders.

When Tony and I first met, we immediately recognized that we had more in common than a first name; we also shared a vision of how the realms of business, communication, leadership, and learning should work. From Tony's vantage point at ASTD, he had a vision of elevating workplace learning to the point where it was a major strategic driver in every organization in the world. I had dedicated my business life (at that point) to teaching Presentation Mastery™ to top achievers and their organizations as a way to boost success. With this book, we wanted to bring those two complementary worldviews together to provide professionals of all kinds with strategies to accelerate their own professional success and the success of others. We also wanted to take giant strides toward revolutionizing how learning in the workplace is perceived, developed, and implemented.

What does the book say?

The book focuses on communication, because much of the frustration learning or training professionals encounter in their job stems from an inability to communicate the value of learning initiatives to the people who need to understand it the most: the executive-level decision makers.

It's not just about developing great programs and measuring outcomes; it's about managing expectations and communicating results in ways that top executives see as meaningful and impactful. It means speaking the language of business, not the language of trainers. Most important, it means making a direct connection between training and performance initiatives and the strategic objectives and key measures of the organization.

Whether you're selling the value of training from inside or outside an organization, the key issue is still the same: What should you say and do to get the outcome you want? Through the use of Presentation Mastery™ principles, we arm the learning and training professional with the knowledge that you can help your organization make wise decisions that will lead down a rewarding path toward prosperity.

How will the book help you?

One of the concepts we wanted to emphasize to the world is that learning has a seat at the table and can speak at the full board level. Training and learning in the workplace are often undervalued, and as a result they are usually among the first assets to be eliminated when companies are downsizing. We make the case that learning is a strategic asset to an organization, so we wrote this book to give our insights on how learning has such an enormous impact on the success of a company.

We developed a five-part mnemonic model to help you think about how to develop, articulate, and link learning in any organization. It's called the SPEAK model, because communication is at its core:

Strategy: As a learning professional who wants to play an active business role, you need to develop a deep understanding of organizational strategy and help link that knowledge with the practical means for attaining it. If you want to serve an organization better, you must know precisely what its strategic objectives are and devote yourself to finding ways to achieve them. Your commitment must be equal to or greater than that of the CEO, because the CEO only demands results; you are responsible for delivering them.

Preparation, **P**ractice, **P**ersonalization:

Preparation: Presentation Masters are always gathering stories and anecdotes that might sharpen their message, reading books and magazines to keep current in their industry, organizing websites and articles for future use, and generally being a sponge for any kind of information that can help them communicate to their audiences. For formal presentations, they go over every detail of their presentation and leave nothing to chance. They research their audience thoroughly, tailor their message accordingly, do their best to anticipate any questions or issues that may crop up, and have answers ready, just in case.

Practice:

Masters embrace a daily regimen of disciplines to help them hone their communication skills. They continually practice their craft, paying close attention to how they use all types of communication, including phone, email, meetings, seminars, web conferencing, and videoconferencing.

Personalization:

Much of professional life is about working with, for, or through other people, so knowing how to build strong personal relationships is central to success. Masters know this, so they try to personalize their communication as much as possible.

Execution: Superior strategy and preparation are useless without great execution. When presenting learning, great execution means having all the little things you've done over the weeks and months add up to a successful outcome. It means paying attention to detail, devoting yourself to excellence, and working hard every day to do the best job you can. Execution is quality in action. Without it, everything else tends to fall apart.

Accountability: An important part of the proactive learning professional's job is to help develop effective and accurate measurement tools and to insist on having metrics that accurately track and report learning's value to the enterprise. Being accountable to the organization in this way is an important step in the quest for business respectability. Only by making learning's value known on the balance sheet will that seat at the table ever start to feel comfortable.

Knowledge: Learning how an organization learns (how the organization processes information to achieve the most competitive, profitable outcome possible) is an important part of the learning professional's job. It's no longer enough to develop great content that meets an organization's surface needs; the learning professional must also be deeply aware of how an organization functions at an organic level in terms of its people, culture, attitudes, politics, etc. Then, the professional must translate that knowledge into effective learning solutions.

Learning is a huge strategic asset to an organization, and it should be looked at accordingly. We published this book to reinforce that reality, because it's overlooked by so many.

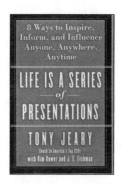

BOOK 31
LIFE IS A SERIES OF PRESENTATIONS

Your life largely consists of interactions with the people around you. Think about all the opportunities you have every day to connect with and communicate your thinking to others and, perhaps, win people over to your point of view. The way you present your thoughts and ideas to people—from your colleagues at work to your spouse or kids, and even the person waiting on you at the grocery store—could have a profound effect on the shape of your life. This book will teach you easy-to-use skills that can change the way you approach every interaction. The eight essential presentation practices we share will allow you to master any exchange, whether it involves a roomful of colleagues, a small group, or just one other person.

I was in L.A. at the Book Expo of America (BEA) trade show about fifteen years ago when I visited a literary publicist's booth and dropped my business card into a fishbowl to enter their drawing for a free coaching session. A few days later, a lady named Kim Dower called me and said, "You've won a free media coaching session. I know you're in the same business, so you probably don't want it, but I wanted to let you know you'd won." I said, "I think I'll take it." She said, "Well, then you'll have to fly to California." So I flew to California

Kim, owner of Kim-from-L.A. Literary & Media Services, is an incredible public relations agent for authors, and she has exceptional talent for helping people present well on the radio. (Visit her website at www.kimfromla.com.) At one point during our coaching session, she said, "Tony, what you're really about is 'life is a series of presentations.'" That concept resonated with me, and I played it out in my workshops and talks for the next several months. Six months went by, and I called her and said, "Kim, let's do a best-selling book with that title." She was wowed. I said, "It was your title, and I'd love to have you co-author with me." She said, "Great!"

We struggled to write the proposal, so our agent called in a third author, Joel Fishman, who was formerly with Doubleday, and asked him to write it. The proposal ended up being a sixty-five-page masterpiece that attracted eight publishers. After an all-day auction, we ended up getting almost a quarter-of-a million-dollar advance from Simon & Schuster, and we worked a sweet deal with them to simultaneously launch the audio, as well.

Life is a Series of Presentations launched to become an instant best-seller and was eventually published in several different languages. About a year ago, Daymond John, of the critically acclaimed and multi-Emmy®-Award-winning reality show *Shark Tank*, hailed it as one of the top six business books everyone should read (right up there with Napoleon Hill's bestseller, *Think and Grow Rich*). I was at a wedding when I found out about the endorsement. Friends were texting me saying, "You're on *Shark Tank*! You're on *Shark Tank*!" to which I would reply, "Nope, I'm at a wedding." This hilarious exchange went back and forth for quite some time until I finally came to realize what they were talking about. *Life is a Series of Presentations* was heralded on a show watched by

Shark Tank's Daymond John recommends Tony's thirty-first book *Life is a Series of Presentations* as a must-read.

millions of people. It was an unexpected and incredible honor to be recognized alongside a classic in the field and by such an esteemed entrepreneur.

What does the book say?

Part One of the book introduces three core concepts for making effective presentations:

1. The psychology of persuasion and influence
2. The principles of Neuro-Linguistic Programming (NLP), which enable people to communicate more effectively at the unconscious level (My clients today often ask that I teach them NLP. It would be powerfully effective for your sales organization to understand and utilize what I've written about it in this first section of the book.)
3. The impact of *Mastery* and how to define your *Presentation Universe*, another process I've developed as a way to strategically get your arms around all your presentations

In Part Two, we set out the eight essential practices of successful presentations—the IPRESENT model—that I've personally tested and proven when presenting to tens of thousands of people and taught to CEOs and high-level achievers across the globe.

How will the book help you?

Foreseeing that the reader's most valuable takeaway from the book would be the eight essential practices of successful presentations, we reinforced their learning by working them into a mnemonic model called IPRESENT:

I   **I**nvolve your audience

P   **P**repare your audience

R   **R**esearch your presentation arsenal

E   **E**xplain "why" before planning "how"

S   **S**tate management: achieve proper mental states

E   **E**liminate "unknowns" by turning them into "knowns"

N   k**N**ow your audience

T   **T**ailor the presentation throughout to keep your audience focused

This book continues today as my flagship book. It covers my methodology of Presentation Mastery™ and is the most popular and impactful of all twenty-six of my books on presentations—a solid must-read.

BOOK 32
PURPOSE-FILLED
PRESENTATIONS

I authored this work for pastors to give to their congregations. Whether you've been asked to lead a small group or make a presentation in front of your church, there are people who need to hear what you have to say. Your message may not get through, though, if you find your knees are knocking louder than you're talking. Worse yet, your lack of confidence in your speaking ability may silence your story altogether by forcing you to shirk away from the very opportunity God brings to you.

Even if you've been involved in ministry for years, you've likely discovered that the delivery can be just as important as the message. Whether you're a novice or a veteran, you may be keenly aware you have room to grow. There's no doubt that your message is essential— you just need your audience to understand how truly important it is. If you're hungry to improve your delivery, you're in good company. Many people in the church today have incredible insight and amazing experiences, yet they just don't know how to really reach their audiences with the message. I offer this book to help change that.

When the idea for this book was conceived, I was coaching my friend Larry Carpenter, who at that time was president of Standard Publishing, one of the oldest and largest publishers of Christian resources in the nation. Larry recognized a real need for helping volunteers within the church gain confidence and credibility in the area of presentations. When he saw that I, too, had a passion in that area, he suggested we publish a book to fit that need, so we made a deal.

Too often, Christian training falls short of preparing volunteers to fulfill the charge God has given them. Churches are full of earnest followers of Christ who are called and willing to deliver God's message through the various venues of the church. However, many of them lack the communication skills and confidence they need to step up to the plate. Since communication has been my life's work, I decided to share my expertise so those volunteers could effectively communicate his message—whether they're encouraging someone, leading a small group, sharing their testimony, or even delivering a sermon. I've helped thousands of CEOs, corporate leaders, and business people on all levels master the art of effective presentations, yet my heart continually goes out to those in the local church who need a boost of confidence to become all God created them to be.

What does the book say?

Purpose-Filled Presentations is a communication guide that helps ministry leaders and volunteers in delivering a variety of effective presentations within the body of Christ. In the first part of the book, we teach basic communication skills that apply across the board for all communicators. You'll discover my *Seven Steps to Effective Presentations*, which teach the basics of Presentation Mastery™, as well as tips on how to move from nervous to natural. Then you'll find best practices on how to strategically prepare for virtually any type of presentation, and you'll learn how to engage your audience to create a winning environment.

The second part of the book relates the *Seven Steps to Effective Presentations* to nine specific scenarios, or areas of service, within the church:

- Sharing your testimony
- Hosting a worship service
- Leading and empowering small groups
- Maximizing teaching opportunities
- Training others
- Leading a great meeting
- Interacting with the media
- Reaching out to others
- Creating great first impressions

How will the book help you?

While helping thousands of people over the years strengthen their presentation skills, I developed what I call the *Seven Steps to Effective Presentations*. Following these seven steps will help you make a powerful and lasting impact in whatever ministry (or business) role you serve:

1. Clarify your objectives
2. Define your audience
3. Gather content
4. Maximize preparation
5. Open well
6. Engage your audience
7. Close with action

This is a great tool for developing and honing your presentation skills to become a more confident, effective ambassador for Christ. Whether you're a church leader or a volunteer, you can use these principles to make a lasting difference in your church and ministry.

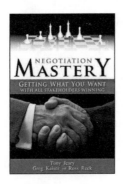

BOOK 33
NEGOTIATION MASTERY

Do you want to achieve dramatic results in both your personal and professional lives? Do you want to be that person who takes charge and makes things happen rather than following the crowd? If you answered yes to these questions, you may aspire to be a Master Negotiator—one who can achieve far beyond what most people would consider acceptable or good by applying the best practices and distinctions we share in this book.

I joined up with two friends, Greg Kaiser and Ross Reck, to write a book for people who want to strategically and proactively create win-win-win situations by applying the concepts of clarity, focus, and execution to any event that involves negotiation.

What does the book say?

Negotiation Mastery shows you how to turn the people who stand between you and success or failure into enduring allies and partners who are excited about helping you achieve dramatic results. What sets Master Negotiators apart is the way they *think*, which in turn determines how they act.

How will the book help you?

Master Negotiators understand that dramatic results don't just happen. They're achieved by executing a well-constructed negotiation plan—a plan based on the fact that negotiation is all about people, and that people are motivated by their self-interest. In other words, it must be a win-win-win plan.

The four steps that Master Negotiators use for constructing a win-win-win plan are:

1. Determine your self-interest—what really matters to you?
2. Identify the people who stand between you and success or failure.
3. Determine their self-interest.
4. Design a strategy to connect their self-interest with yours.

To illustrate this concept in the book, we told the story of Joe Girard, who made it into the *Guinness Book of World Records* as the world's "Number One New Car Salesman." Joe sold 1,425 new cars in one year, which was a phenomenal individual accomplishment! So how did he do it? Was he some kind of hard-charging dynamo or a workaholic who worked sixteen hours a day at full speed? Worse yet, was he a fast-talking sales type who wouldn't take no for an answer? Actually, he was none of the above. He was just an ordinary man who was quite laid back.

For some insight, let's look at a breakdown of Joe's sales the year he was included in the *Guinness Book of World Records.* That year, 65 percent of Joe's sales were to repeat customers, and the other 35 percent came from customers who had been *referred* from Joe's repeat customers. So how many cars did Joe actually sell that year? The answer, amazingly, is *none! His customers sold them for him!* Joe was a master at getting his customers excited about going the extra mile for him—he was a Master Negotiator.

When people asked Joe how he achieved such dramatic results, he would come back with something like, "There are no secrets; you just have to do certain things right. First, you have to get to know your customers. I sell Chevrolets. Who buys Chevrolets?" In Joe's own words, it was "your average Joe," the person who goes to work every day.

Once he got to know the average Joe, he quickly discovered they don't want to pay the cheapest price they can for a car. They don't mind paying a fair price; they just don't want to feel that someone has taken advantage of them. Their most important concern, though, is that they want to buy a car from a salesperson they can trust.

Joe said that in order to give the customers what they want, "I stand in front of my product as well as behind it." In other words, before you could buy one car from Joe, you first had to buy Joe. He would not let you out of his office until he turned you into a friend. Then, if you had a problem with the service department after you bought a car from Joe, he would fight on your behalf with the mechanics, the dealership, and even the factory to make sure you were treated fairly.

As Joe put it, "If you think the sale ends when, as they say in the car business, 'you see the customer's taillights,' you're going to lose more sales than you ever dreamed of. But if you understand how selling can be a continuous process that never ends, then you are going to make it to the big time."

Joe's consistent execution of his win-win-win plan resulted in thousands of customers waiting in line to buy a car from him. This not only put Joe in the *Guinness Book of World Records*, it also made him a very wealthy man.

BOOK 34
THE 180 RULE FOR
GETTING RESULTS FASTER

The 180 Rule Series is a collection of books designed to demonstrate how the unique 180 Rule problem-solving technique can be used effectively in multiple subject areas and disciplines. The premise of the series is that you can learn how to use your natural tendencies of negativity to drive your personal and professional success. Each book in the series focuses on the expertise of a nationally recognized expert and combines their wealth of knowledge and experience with this surprisingly simple technique.

The 180 Rule methodology was created by my good friend Al Lucia, who asked me to contribute my expertise in getting results faster to the series.

What does the book say?
The 180 Rule is a methodology that embraces the reality that new ideas or concepts are often met with negative feedback (the

"Negativity Bias"). Harnessing the power of the Negativity Bias helps you achieve the results you're looking for; in other words, coming up with what will *not* work gives you a roadmap to use for what *will* work, or at least get you started on the right track.

To get the superior results you seek, I encourage you to employ my *Strategic Acceleration* methodology of clarity, focus, and execution. That methodology, combined with the 180 Rule technique, can be a complete way of thinking and problem solving.

When you <u>identify</u> and <u>analyze</u> roadblocks that impede your vision, you'll have true clarity about how to get results. <u>Developing solutions</u> to those roadblocks allows you to focus on activities that really matter (*High Leverage Activities*, or HLAs). And having a strong <u>action plan</u> that details <u>implementation</u>, <u>follow-up</u>, and <u>measurement</u> will help you execute for real success and tangible, positive results.

How will this book help you?

Here's how the 180 Rule, combined with the *Strategic Acceleration* methodology, works to identify and analyze the root issues that are keeping you from living in *Mastery*:

> **Clarity**: Determine where you are, where you want to be, and what's stopping you from getting the results you want:
>
> 1. Firmly fix in your mind the goal or task you want to accomplish (<u>problem identification</u>).
> 2. Turn your task or goal around 180 degrees and make a new mission statement that is the complete opposite of your true mission. Allow the natural tendency to sabotage an idea (the Negativity Bias) kick in. You should then be able to easily come up with all the things you would need to do to accomplish your new 180 Rule statement (<u>problem analysis</u>).
>
> **Focus**: Get what you want by concentrating on activities that really matter, or what I call *High Leverage Activities* (HLAs).
>
> 1. Prioritize your list (<u>problem solution</u>).
>
> **Execution**: Deploy a plan to accomplish everything necessary to get results and measure your success.

1. Ask yourself how many of the action steps you're doing or could be perceived to be doing (<u>implementation</u>).
2. Continue with the 180 Rule Problem-Solving Technique to bring into focus what will not work (<u>follow-up and measurement</u>).
3. Create an action plan for success with a clear understanding of what will *not* work fixed in your mind (<u>action plan</u>).

Clarity and focus provide your plan of "what" and "how"; however, when it's time to get things done, it's all about actually doing it! This might sound simple, and yet this is where you're going to spend most of your time. Approaching it by being well-prepared and using the 180 Rule technique will make a difference toward your results.

BOOK 35
ULTIMATE HEALTH

Ultimate Health is one of the most important books you could ever read. You'll discover how to create a life of vitality, strength, and energy, with a preventive mindset that enhances longevity. You'll learn why food is medicine, spirituality matters, and how a positive emotional outlook can add years to your life and life to your years. You'll gain knowledge about the right habits, foods, vitamins, nutrients and exercise that will allow you to turn back the hands of time and regain a more youthful life. I hope you'll join me in seeking ultimate health!

When I turned fifty, I looked at myself in the mirror and didn't like what I saw. Not long after that, I had a breakfast one morning with my friend and client, Texas State Congressman Ron Simmons, who had lost seventy pounds since I had seen him last. He looked terrific! I said, "Ron, what's up with your looking so good?"

"I learned that once you turn fifty, it's not about exercise," he said.

"It's not?"

"No, it's about what you eat." (I've since learned that what he said wasn't exactly accurate; it's really about what you absorb rather than what you eat.)

Then he said, "Tony, do you realize the GI content of the three glasses of orange juice you just drank?"

"No, Ron, I don't know what GI means."

"Glycemic Index."

"What's Glycemic Index?"

"That's the sugar content." Then he basically said, "The higher the GI, the more fat you store, and you just slammed down three big glasses. In fact, do you know how many calories you just drank?"

"No."

"There are about 250 calories in each glass; that's 750 calories you took in before you even started eating that greasy bacon!"

If he was trying to shock me, it worked! In fact, that conversation caused an immediate pattern interrupt in my life. My parents taught me that orange juice is healthy; unfortunately, they were wrong!

I suddenly realized that, like many people, I had gone through most of my life without even knowing how my body works or how food works in the body. How about you? Have you neglected your health, as well?

Determined to rectify the situation, I went on a tenacious search to understand my body so I could make better decisions from that point forward. I studied and learned all the distinctions I could find about truly living healthy, and I put them to work. Within a couple of years, I had dropped thirty pounds and regained more energy and vitality! I eventually lost forty pounds, reduced my body fat to 11 percent, and shaved 6.5 inches from my waist. I couldn't believe the difference in the way I felt, and I wanted to share what I had learned with all of my high-achieving clients. So I teamed up with two doctors from the famous Cooper Clinic, Dr. Rick Wilson and Dr. Jennifer Engels, along with my good friend Tammy Kling, to author the book *Ultimate Health*.

This book is not about me. It's actually about you! In its pages, we encourage you to not only survive, but to thrive, learn, and grow.

We want to help you transform each day into an abundant life full of healthy choices and outcomes.

What does the book say?

We start the book with the *Ultimate Health Assessment*—a three-minute evaluation of the twenty areas that have the most impact on your health. A chapter is devoted to each of the twenty areas. When you identify an area of weakness in the assessment, you can go directly to the chapter that covers that particular topic and learn how to turn that weakness into a strength.

Ultimate Health was written to inspire people to gain clarity about what they want and how healthy they want to become. At the time it was written, I was in the process of proving that I could reduce my body age from a fifty-year-old to a twenty-five-year-old. My goal was to demonstrate that most people can achieve whatever results they really wanted in the area of their health, and I accomplished that goal.

How will the book help you?

One of the big takeaways from the book is the concept that everyone has three different types of ages: your mental age, your physical age, and your chronological age. Your chronological age is what you celebrate with your birthdays; your mental age is how fun you are; and your physical age has to do with your cellular makeup, which is determined by multiple bio-markers that can be measured inside and outside of your body.

We've included the *Ultimate Health Assessment,* which is the first step toward discovering the areas you need to improve or modify in order to live in ultimate health.

Ultimate Health Assessment

Rate yourself on a scale of 1 to 5, with 5 being the highest, on your current effectiveness in each area.

#	Category	Description	Rating
1.	Lifestyle	How are you living your life? Managing balance, managing risks, resting, saying no enough, and exercise all make up your overall living routine. Are your habits supporting your health?	
2.	Mental Management	What goes on in your mind truly impacts your health. Assess your own self-talk, your daily attitude, your beliefs about being healthy and not getting sick, and your willingness to release grudges and forgive, while focusing on the positives. Filter the input you receive from sources such as news, media, or even negative people.	
3.	Ultimate Longevity	Do you have a great team of health professionals that know you and guide you? Family doctor? Nutritionist? Dentist? Do you have regular checkups and vaccines? Do your behaviors align with real health?	
4.	Stress Management	Are you managing anxiety? Are you meditating? Relaxing enough? Is your life aligned with your values? Have you set up harmony in your life so things run as smoothly as possible? Is your pace of life contributing to or detracting from your overall well-being?	

(Continued)

#	Category	Description	Rating
5.	Immune System	Your immune system protects you. It detects potential harm and helps your body react. Are you helping yourself? Are you resting at the right time, for example, when you sense your body needs it to ensure you stay well? Are you maintaining good hygiene; protecting against harmful bacteria; and practicing plain and simple cleanliness, such as washing your hands enough and avoiding being in contact with the wrong things, in order to support your wellness?	
6.	Testing	Early detection is great common sense in today's world of information. How is your discipline on staying current on screenings, blood work reviews, EKGs, MRIs, hormone testing, and urinalysis—even full-body skin screenings every few years? There are many simple things we can do to be proactive. Are you taking advantage of these options?	
7.	Exercise	Physical exercise matters—regular, frequent, and ongoing. Resistance exercise, cardiovascular exercise (aerobics), balance, and stretching all promote a better-operating body.	
8.	Oral	Obviously, it is important to keep your mouth clean. Are you brushing enough? Flossing enough? Going for regular check-ups?	

(Continued)

#	Category	Description	Rating
9.	Eyes/ Vision	Are you protecting your eyes from sunlight and eating the things that help prevent cataracts later in life? Are you going for regular checkups? Do you wear eye protection when doing certain types of work around the house? All these factors add up to promoting this key component to your body's overall health.	
10.	Toxin Management	What's around you can get in your body through your skin, what you breathe, and what you eat. Toxins are potentially hazardous substances that can place an extra toll on your body, such as forcing your liver and kidneys to work overtime as they filter fluids. Are you protecting yourself like you could or should?	
11.	Hormone Management	A hormone is a chemical released by a cell or a gland in one part of your body that sends out messages that affect cells in other parts of your body. In essence, it's a chemical messenger that transports a signal from one cell to another. Have you tested your chemical balances (estrogen, testosterone, thyroid, DHEA, etc.)? Are you supplementing where you should?	
12.	Vitamins	A vitamin is an organic compound required as a vital nutrient in tiny amounts by an organism. Vitamins help your body function optimally. Are you managing your regular intake, testing so you know, and living daily with the right balances in your body?	

(Continued)

#	Category	Description	Rating
13.	Caloric Management	A calorie is a unit of energy. It is a measure of the energy we generate with every task we do, as well as a measure of the energy delivered by a food we eat. How well do you know your body and how you balance what you eat versus what you need to perform? Being in tune and knowing this can allow you to make better daily choices . . . and live better!	
14.	Ear, Nose, and Throat	Preventive testing is important for the ear, nose, and throat, the same as for the rest of your body. It is important to protect your hearing and ear canal from foreign objects and loud noises. Are you maintaining good hygiene? Are you getting checked regularly?	
15.	Food	Food is any substance consumed to provide nutritional support for your body. It is usually of plant or animal origin, and contains essential nutrients, such as carbohydrates, fats, proteins, vitamins, and minerals. It is what we consume in an effort to produce energy, maintain life, and stimulate growth. How is your balance? How is your mix? Are you eating throughout the day to promote good metabolism? Do you eat slowly and chew well in order to promote good digestion? Do you make healthy choices such as limiting the fried, processed, and high-sugar foods you eat?	

(Continued)

#	Category	Description	Rating
16.	Skin	Your skin is the largest organ in your body. It acts as an external filter and can even provide many clues about the condition of your body internally. Are you protecting it like you should from ultraviolet rays or from harmful chemicals that can get into your body? Do you get full-body skin screenings to detect cancers or other harmful things that need attention in order to ensure your ultimate health? Skin cancer is the most common cancer there is.	
17.	Fluids	Consuming adequate amounts of water is critical to maintaining ultimate health. Do you drink enough water each day? Do you manage your alcohol intake? Do you drink too much soda or other high-sugar drinks?	
18.	Emotions	Emotion is a complex psycho-physiological experience of your state of mind as you interact with internal and external influences. How are your mood, temperament, personality, disposition, and motivation? All these elements matter; all impact the way our bodies perform.	
19.	Sleep	Sleep suspends the sensory activity of nearly all voluntary muscles. It accentuates the growth and rejuvenation of the immune, nervous, skeletal, and muscular systems. Are you getting enough sleep? Is it good sleep?	

(Continued)

#	Category	Description	Rating
20.	Spiritual wellness	Your spiritual wellness is to a large degree reflective of your worldview. Is it egocentric or others oriented? Would others say you display stress tolerance and adequate marginal reserves for life's challenges? What wisdom do you apply to your life situations in order to achieve spiritual balance, peace, and joy?	

Your Total: _____

Interpreting Your Total

A 100 is exceptional—and exceptionally rare. This is not designed to be a scientific assessment but an awareness tool.

5-20: Red flag
21-55: Average
56-80: Above average
80-100: Excellent

Take action in the areas in which you need to improve. Take charge of your health and learn in the book about the steps you can take to live a healthier and more energetic life.

BOOK 36
LEADERSHIP 25

Let's face it: In today's incredibly fast-paced and increasingly competitive world, leadership is a results contest. We've talked often in this book about clarity, focus, and execution, and they are more important than ever when it comes to your effectiveness as a leader. In my experience, winners who get consistent, real results start with a powerful strategic plan fueled by a clear vision, constant reevaluation and adjustment, true insight into what's really happening around them, and a supportive team focused on executing and bringing out the best in their leadership. Where do you stand in that process?

I'm a huge believer in assessments. In my opinion, they're one of the most strategic tools you can use to improve your results. Many people go through life without assessing the things that are important—like their marriage, their parenting, their health, or their leadership qualities. Since they don't even know what they don't know, they certainly don't have the means to improve their results in those areas.

What does the book say?

From all my years of coaching the world's high achievers, I developed an assessment tool strategically designed for top leaders. It's been updated and refined over the years, resulting in this *Leadership 25* book that outlines the areas where leaders need to focus to be most effective. It's easy to use and was intentionally designed for the busy leader. It will uncover *Blind Spots* and often reframe how you invest your time, help you better see the world around you, and accelerate your success.

One of the distinctions you may not have thought about is positively touching your *People of Influence* (POI)—those individuals who have the most influence on your results. Strong leaders know who really matters in their lives along the path to results. These *People of Influence* can make all the difference in your level of success, and they deserve to be intentionally nurtured. What does that look like? It could be keeping in touch, remembering their birthdays by sending a personalized gift, or doing *Favors in Advance* (one of my personal standards). Creating wins for these special people in your life will inevitably create wins for you—immediately, midterm, or down the road.

How will the book help you?

Take the Leadership Assessment below to determine the three to five areas you're most intentional about improving.

Executive Focus and Clarity	Rating 1-4*
1. A powerful and well-thought-out *Strategic Plan* tied to a simple, well-thought-out vision (and a system for ensuring all team members understand and are reminded constantly, to ensure focus). CLARITY!	
2. *Vision Model/Tools:* A visual cascading tool(s) to complement the vision of your organization's priorities	
3. Annual *SWOT/MOLO:* Evaluating your strengths and weaknesses and what you want to do more of and less of, two or three times a year	

(Continued)

4. *Benchmarking:* Looking at best practices, modeling part or all to grow your effectiveness	
5. *Competitive/Comparison Matrix:* Top people know their competition well and document and inform their teams as needed, keeping up with trends, sweet spots, and industry best practices.	
Personal Development & Strength in Decision Making	
6. *Strategic Presence,* or a strategic approach to your *Professional Brand* (inside the organization and outside, including investors/the street, new team members, other departments, and of course clients and customers)	
7. *Health/Energy Management* (Diet, Timing, and Stress): It's not just about 168 hours in a week; it's about being at peak for the top opportunities. No health, no performance. Period.	
8. *Feeding your mind:* Innovating, growing, learning (reading, listening, being coached so you consistently model self-improvement for those you lead); avoiding stagnation with constant fresh inputs	
9. *Managing HLAs:* Understand prioritization—doing what matters most	
10. *Reality vs. Numbers:* As a successful leader, you measure but also know what the metrics mean (CSFs or KPIs)	
Presentation/Communication	
11. *Meeting Effectiveness:* Ensure all meeting invites and actual meetings themselves have strong objectives, a good agenda, the right people there, and good clear actions at the end of each meeting	

(Continued)

12. *Presentation Ready:* Have tools and messaging thought through for new contacts, analysts, board, impromptu opportunities, town halls, etc.; understand your *Presentation Universe* so you're clear on all the types of presentations that impact your success; have extreme clarity between you and your team, with constant links back to your vision and strategic priorities	
13. *Personality Profile Management:* Understand and utilize personality profiling (e.g., DISC) for all hiring, motivating, negotiating, etc.; exchange with your team, so they know yours and you know theirs	
14. *Information Management:* Getting the information you need quickly and on a regular basis so you're in a strong position to make better decisions; develop a team to constantly feed you new information	
15. Team Huddles: Consistent habit of collaborating your close team around you (by phone or in person), in order to have synchronized focus and clarity of priorities	
Leading a Strong Team	
16. Performance Standards: For yourself and those around you, especially your direct reports, which helps ensure expectations are met and shortens the learning curve for new people joining your team	
17. Mentoring: For up and comers, truly supporting those you lead (bench strength)	
18. People of Influence (POI): Touching consistently those who have the biggest influence on your objectives	
19. Advisors: Special teams to help guide, stimulate, and bring fresh ideas and perspectives—informal board, close team (form a team around you—executive assistant, coach, mentors, colleagues, readers, financial support [e.g., CPA, etc.])	

(Continued)

20. Culture: Team synergy constantly improving, trust, accountability, and open communication	
People Power	
21. Assistant Effectiveness: Personal staff, including executive assistant, and *Life Team* (e.g., presentation management, travel, organization list) (Email us at info@ tonyjeary.com for our Executive Assistant 50 list.)	
22. Time Saving Team: Utilize a driver, researchers for things like Smart Reports, and travel agent who knows you well, to save your time and energy so you can negotiate, inspire, strategize, and lead more effectively	
23. Networking/Connections: Have a system for building and nourishing new and existing contacts	
24. Social Capital: Doing positive things for people in your world in advance in order to have a "bank account" to request favors and actions, even ideas and reviews in the future	
25. Stuff Management: Handling inflow, sorting, organizing, and good retrieval	
Total: _____	

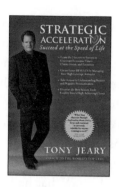

BOOK 37
STRATEGIC ACCELERATION
SUCCEED AT THE SPEED OF LIFE
(MY SIGNATURE BOOK)

Getting superior results at the fastest rate possible is critical to success in today's ultra-competitive, breakneck world. Has it been your experience that this hectic speed of life can make it easy to become distracted by things that make you less effective? If your answer is yes, then my *Strategic Acceleration* methodology presented in this book will help you get more clear, stay more focused, and more efficiently execute *High Leverage Activities* (HLAs) that bring you the results and success you want—faster.

As I was sitting in first class on a plane going to Detroit in 1994, I saw Zig Ziglar sitting across the aisle. I went over and introduced myself and thanked him for the impact he had made on my life. He introduced me to the man traveling with him, Jim Norman, who was the president of his company. They were on their way to Detroit, as well, for a speaking engagement with Chrysler. I knelt down in the aisle, and for the rest of the flight I shared with them insights I had gained over the previous three years about Chrysler's corporate structure, their needs, and their vision for the future.

They began to understand that my niche was helping organizations grow and that their niche was helping individuals grow (personal development). As a result, they ended up hiring me to help them get into corporations, and we became great friends. Both Jim and Zig became mentors to me, and the more I got to know Jim, the more impressed I was with him. What he had done to impact Zig and his thinking was phenomenal. I started envisioning Jim's becoming my president one day.

As I mentioned in the introduction, when Jim resigned as Zig's president in 1996, I literally started begging him to come on as my president. He turned down my request; however, he did agree to be my coach. Ten years went by. In 2006 he finally agreed to become my president, and the first thing he did was interview our top thirty clients to find out what value I was really giving them—why they were investing big money and flying their teams in to my estate to spend time with me. Here's what he came back and told me: "You're helping people think. Thinking's not easy. In fact, it's hard, and most people don't do it enough. You show people that the way to think better is to gain *clarity* of their visions (what they want and where they want to go), and then how they can better *focus* their efforts and the efforts of their team so they can *execute* with accountability to get the right results faster."

As a result of his findings, Jim and I wrote a little book called *The Passport to Strategic Acceleration*. We printed 10,000 copies and mailed out 5,000 of them to various organizations. A few days later I got a call from the Sergeant at Arms for the US Senate, who basically said, "Tony, we need clarity, focus, and execution up here in the Senate." So I flew to Washington and worked with the 170 people on the Senate's management team. They got fired up over the clarity, focus, and execution formula—so much so, in fact, that I flew back home and said to Jim, "I believe we're onto something here. We need to get with my agent and write a best seller."

In 2006 we published *Strategic Acceleration*, my signature book that introduces the *Strategic Acceleration* formula of *Clarity, Focus, and Execution*. Since that time, I've been able to help people around the globe, the world's top high achievers, get better results faster through my methodologies and best practices, my war (tool) chest, and my hand-selected team members.

By the time we wrote the book, I had started coaching the president of The News Group, the company that puts the books and the magazines on newsstands everywhere, including at the airports. We decided to make it an airport book so they could help us with distribution, and also because we knew it would be valuable to airline passengers who are typically looking for an easy read that can be applied to both the personal and professional sides of their life. This book is both—its concepts apply about 60 percent to the professional side and about 40 percent to the personal side.

What does the book say?

Strategic Acceleration provides a simple, strategic thought process that will transform the way you think, live, and work. Both individuals and organizations have two basic needs in order to be successful at the very highest level—the need for speed and the need for results! Things are changing so rapidly in today's world that you need to have a way to not only cope with these changes, but to also use them to your advantage. There are three enemies to speed and results:

1. The absence of clarity
2. Lack of focus
3. Poor execution

The formula of *Clarity, Focus, and Execution* that I've developed in my life's work dramatically impacts the ability of a person, a small team, a large group, or even a whole organization, to get more results in an accelerated format. The formula is founded upon a system that will show you how to think differently, because changing your thinking is going to change your results.

Clarity: Understanding your vision and knowing exactly
                 what you want. There's a pulling power that comes
                 from clarity.

Focus: The opposite of distraction; concentrating on what
                 really matters (*High Leverage Activities*) and filtering
                 out what doesn't.

Execution: We all have to take action (ideally, in strategic
                 alignment with your vision) to get accelerated results
                 with powerful accountability.

How will the book help you?

Since we came out with *Strategic Acceleration* in 2006, we've heard from top achievers all over the world that the most valuable takeaway from the book was the concept of *High Leverage Activities* (HLAs). No single skill or habit has a more powerful impact on results than the ability to eliminate distractions and focus on your *High Leverage Activities*. Success truly hinges on the ability to cut through the clutter, drown out the noise, and focus on the *High Leverage Activities* that are the backbone of reaching your vision.

The second biggest takeaway or overall win for readers is the distinction that you can and must be *Intentionally Strategic* about virtually everything you do, including your HLA's. As you can tell from the name *Strategic Acceleration*, strategy is obviously the key to optimizing the *Clarity, Focus, and Execution* formula, and that applies to your personal life as well as your business. I encourage you to identify HLAs in both areas and be *Intentionally Strategic* about focusing on them to get the best results. I believe you can be *Intentionally Strategic* about your health (as you can see in my book *Ultimate Health*, Book 35); you can be *Intentionally Strategic* about raising your kids (see my book *Strategic Parenting*, Book 41); you can be *Intentionally Strategic* about your relationships (see my book *Rich Relationships, Rich Life*, Book 44); and you can be *Intentionally Strategic* about getting advice (see my book *Advice Matters*, Book 45). The very best top achievers, those who have extraordinary results in their life, are *Intentionally Strategic* about focusing on the *High Leverage Activities* that will bring them superior results in all areas of their lives.

Expanded Thinking

Since the book was published we've coined another term, *Low Leverage Activities* (LLAs)—those activities that have the least amount of return. LLAs are typically task-oriented and often become distractions to what your true focus should be. Remember the time model from Book 4, *How to Gain 100 Extra Minutes a Day*? We all have 168 hours in a week, and taking out 56 hours for sleep and 12 hours for maintenance leaves you with 100 hours. Most people divide that into about 50 hours for personal time and 50 for professional time. How well you strategically manage those 100 hours will determine your results, so think about this: How big a hit is your company taking from the fifteen to thirty hours a week that each team member is potentially wasting on LLAs? Most of the time that's wasted on LLAs is due to poor clarity and lack of focus (including the inability to say no more often). What kind of impact would it make on your results if everyone focused on HLA's rather than LLAs?

BOOK 38
WE'VE GOT TO START MEETING AND EMAILING LIKE THIS

Two of the most common factors preventing positive results in organizations are unproductive meetings and ineffective email communication. Everyone agrees when I share this, and no one is ever surprised. Organizations need to address this. In any given company, people often waste hours a day in these two areas. Most organizations could significantly improve their Return on Investment (ROI) and Return on Effort (ROE) in both areas if they would take my simple yet powerful advice—craft strategic standards for both. Improving meeting and email execution is primarily an awareness issue. That's why this little book has such a dramatic impact! Where does your organization stand on these two issues? Can you see room for improvement?

This book is an updated version of *Too Many Emails*, the book I wrote and licensed to Walmart in 2003. My friend George Lowe and I had been training people on meeting and email practices for years and had seen the results that prove our distinctions work. We decided to co-author yet another book to help people and organizations enhance their meeting and email effectiveness.

What does the book say?

Based on our work over the years with many of the world's largest corporations, we identified these ten meeting best practices and ten email best practices that can revolutionize your culture; dramatically increase your team's results, productivity, and morale; and significantly improve your internal and external communications:

EMAILS: ASSESS YOURSELF

Rate yourself in each area on a scale of 1 to 10:

1. Determine what you want to accomplish		6. Use CC and BCC Carefully	
2. Frontload your emails with action		7. Reduce the volume	
3. Leverage the subject line		8. Get it "good enough" and get it out	
4. Set and follow written standards		9. Think before you hit "send"	
5. Make it easy on the receiver		10. Use the phone	
		Total	

MEETINGS: ASSESS YOURSELF

Rate yourself in each area on a scale of 1 to 10:

1. Set and follow written meeting standards		6. Facilitate results	
2. Define your objectives		7. Take clear and concise action	
3. Involve the right people		8. Conquer conference calls and virtual meetings	
4. Create a timed agenda		9. Develop a clear action plan, then follow up	
5. Manage the details		10. Cascade outcomes to others	
		Total	

How will the book help you?

Enhancing meeting and email effectiveness is so powerful and far-reaching that it often produces a radical transformation that creates and sustains substantial results. When used as a primer to change your organization's culture and habits around meetings and emails, this book can add three to five and even ten hours a week back into every person's schedule. And in today's fast-paced world, that's like gold!

Many company leaders overlook the critical importance of creating standards and training their people on these two important communication areas (and even building the standards into their onboarding process). The amount of waste and weakness in these two areas actually negatively affects a whole culture. People hate waste (as they should), and everyone is maxed out with too many emails. What a difference you could make in your organization if you would implement the practices outlined in this book! You could see improved moral, increased productivity, and more positive results in your organization today!

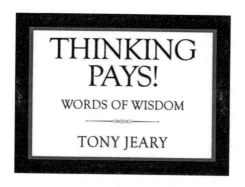

BOOK 39
THINKING PAYS

For many years I've been fascinated with the whole idea of thinking. I've invested my life studying books, audios, and videos and learning from the best minds, researchers, and high achievers. And you know by now that a big part of how we impact our clients—helping them achieve results faster—is by helping them think differently.

Several years ago, I made a list of the one hundred books that have had the most powerful impact on my own life. (Email me at info@tonyjeary.com if you would like a copy of this list.) I realized that many of the books on the list had to do with thinking—books like *As a Man Thinketh*, by James Allen; *Think and Grow Rich*, by Napoleon Hill; *The Power of Positive Thinking*, by Norman Vincent Peale; *The Strangest Secret* (we become what we think about), by Earle Nightingale; *The Magic of Thinking Big*, by David J. Schwartz; and *The Millionaire Mind*, by Thomas J Stanley. When I read Gary Keller's book *The One Thing* a few years later, I realized that my "one thing" is helping people think. I believe I have a God-given talent for encouraging people, and I encourage them to think at a deeper level.

The main theme I teach now and will promote for the rest of my life is being *Intentionally Strategic* about everything, and that starts with thinking. That's been such an overarching theme of my life's work that we began this book talking about it in the introduction, we've talked about it in many of the narratives for these fifty books, and we will end this book talking about it in the conclusion. You may remember that being *Intentionally Strategic* has been one of the biggest takeaways from Book 37, *Strategic Acceleration*. That's the book we published after Jim Norman became my president, when he made me realize that helping people think and be *Intentionally Strategic* is what I do best. Jim is the one who supercharged my thinking on thinking. In fact, thinking has become so prolific in my life and in my life's work that Jim and I decided to write a book together about it. It's called *Thinking: Change Your Thinking, Change Your Results*, and we were only able to complete the first chapter before he passed away. We've capped this *Book of Books* off by including that chapter in the conclusion, because we hope that will be the final and most important thing you take away from everything we've presented in this book.

What does the book say?

This is a coffee-table book with select words of wisdom. My team and I carefully extracted 120 of my most powerful and meaningful quotes from the more than forty books I had published up to that point.

How will the book help you?

We believe these quotes that will give you extraordinary value and impact your results, both personally and professionally.

Here are ten powerful quotes that you can apply to your life and business:

1. Be both strategic and intentional about every single thing you do.
2. Get clear on what you want to have, share, experience, and perhaps more importantly, what you want to become.

3. Go through life with well thought-out and documented values that you can live your life by, and then align your goals and time accordingly.
4. Appreciate what you want more of.
5. Discover and be aware of what others really want and care about.
6. Love your kids with openness, respect, and trust; pray with them daily; share with them; and model what you want them to become.
7. Life changes; enjoy it and work *with* it, not *against* it.
8. We should be intentional about our habits; they produce our life's results.
9. People like to win; help them win, and in return they will help you win.
10. A smile is a powerful thing—it affects how people respond to and are attracted to you, as well as how you feel about yourself.

BOOK 40
BUSINESS GROUND RULES

"Their writings are a success 'playbook' that will raise the performance of top leaders across the business world." Those are the words of Ricky Richardson, the president of TGI Friday's, in his endorsement of *Business Ground Rules*. The book contains the business principles that have transformed hundreds of high-achieving individuals, leaders, entrepreneurs, and companies that both Peter Thomas and I have worked with over the years, and it can transform your life as well.

Mark Pantak, who's been my coach for over thirty years, called me one day about fifteen years ago and said, "Tony, I've found a guy who has more goals than you do." I said, "I doubt it," and he said, "He really does." At the time I had about fifty pages (not *fifty goals*, but *fifty pages of goals*). When Mark told me he could get me a copy of this guy's goals, I said, "That would be wonderful."

Sure enough, the guy had about seventy-five pages of goals, and I was quite impressed. As I started reading his goals, I noticed that they were tied to his values. When your values and your goals are tied together, you can get powerful results! And because his values were so closely aligned with mine, I decided to take about fifty of his seventy-five pages of goals and add them to mine. That gave me one hundred pages of goals—more than any person I'd ever met.

The guy turned out to be Peter Thomas, who has been a serial entrepreneur for more than four decades, specializing in franchising and real estate. He has developed billions of dollars in real estate projects, including shopping centers, apartments, condominiums, and golf courses. He built Century 21 across Canada, setting up over 400 locations, and he developed the Four Seasons Resort in Scottsdale, Arizona. Today I've joined him in investing in and building out Dogtopia, a growing dog spa franchise (see www.dogtopia.com).

I lived Peter's goals, incorporated with mine, for many years, and then Jim and I wrote my book *Strategic Acceleration*. Out of the blue, Peter sent me an email one Saturday about ten years later saying, "Tony, I really like your book *Strategic Acceleration*, and I want to buy a hundred copies." He didn't know at the time that the reason he liked the book so much was because he had been such a big influence in my life. By the time I wrote the book, I had been living his goals for several years, and a lot of his thinking had ended up in *Strategic Acceleration*!

He also shared that he would like to start another big company and that he wanted me to help him with it. He said, "In fact, I have an idea in mind, and I'd like to write another book. If you're interested, give me a call." Of course I was interested! I called him that afternoon, and we talked for three hours. Five minutes into the conversation, he got his wife Rita on the line, and she joined us for the rest of the conversation.

A few weeks later, Peter invited me to visit him on his yacht for a few days. As we started talking about the book, he challenged me to get it written before Christmas. To his surprise, I had brought along my great friend and ghostwriter, Tammy Kling, and we sat down right then and planned the book. We wrote and published it in less than two months. We decided to call the book *Business Ground Rules*, as it would include fifty of his best lessons for success and fifty of mine.

Within an hour of my being on his yacht, he hired me to be his coach for life. Now we get together two or three times a year, often on his yacht, and we mastermind and help each other win. Do you have a few good mastermind partners?

What does the book say?

In order to be really successful in life, you must start with focus and clarity. If you don't have clarity on your values, goals, and dreams, it will be difficult to really get focused, and you won't always get what you want. The 100 lessons for success within the pages of this book will help you gain clarity on what it takes to be extraordinary—both in business and in your life.

How will the book help you?

The wisdom we share in *Business Ground Rules* will transform your thinking, and we hope it will inspire you to take action. Both of us have studied, implemented, refined, lived out, advised, failed at, improved, and documented the distinctions we include in the book.

The book offers one hundred user-friendly strategies/lessons for your business, life, and growth, based on the distinctions, principles, and refinements we've both personally adopted. The contents are divided into twelve categories, and we've selected one sample principle from each category to share with you.

1. Thinking: Avoid Negative Thoughts

    > Have a solution-oriented attitude and a "how do we?" versus a "why we can't?" mindset.

    > —Tony Jeary

    You need to eliminate your negative thoughts in the same way you would take the garbage out when it starts to stink or occupies too much space.

2. Clarity: Utilize the Power of Visualization

    > Visualization is the ability to "see" the end result before you begin.

    > —Peter Thomas

    Successful people create a tangible vision that motivates them toward what they desire to achieve. They understand how important it is to engage the visual aspect of motivating themselves and their teams toward their goals. Visualization is a key aspect of becoming a winner and achieving exactly what you want.

3.   Time: Understand Positive and Negative Procrastination

Live *Production Before Perfection* (PBP). The main idea of PBP is to act first, and get it perfect later. Operating with a PBP mindset helps us flow much more effectively in the fast-paced world we live in today.

—Tony Jeary

People who use planning to avoid action often get tangled in an unhealthy emotional cycle of evaluation and analysis paralysis. Preparation and planning are important, but excessive preparation is nothing more than procrastination—it's that simple.

4.   Strategic: Be Intentional about Everything

Be both strategic and intentional about every single thing you do.

—Tony Jeary

Intentionality exists when you know exactly what you want, and everything flows from that. First, you must know what you really want. Then you can be intentional about taking action.

5.   Focus: Aim for 87 Percent

Don't allow your standards and commitment to mastery to interfere with getting things done; 87% is often good enough. Be okay with it sometimes and move on.

—Peter Thomas

High expectations are great, but there are always other factors in any situation. In most cases, 87 percent will be just as good as 100 or better because of the worrying, stress, and negative energy that come with trying to achieve a perfect score.

6.   Brand: Be Real. People Appreciate Transparency!

Always play with your cards face up.

—Jay Rodgers

This rule isn't just about honesty with others; it's about being honest and true to yourself. Are you really living the life you want to live? If you're not, it can show.

7.   Leadership: Support a High-Energy Culture

High achievers set up systems, people, and processes to help them discover and see distinctions and achieve greater results.

—Tony Jeary

The energy level of the culture around you is a direct result of the core beliefs shared by everyone involved. It has a huge impact on what level of achievement will become reality.

8.   People: Build Relationships and Help Others Win

Sometimes the greatest success can be measured by the number of people you influence and encourage in their pursuit of success.

—Tony Jeary

When you help those around you win, they will, in turn, want to help you win. It's fairly simple to do, and it reaps huge benefits for all stakeholders.

9.   Money: Pay Average Salaries and Higher Bonuses

Strip your company of cash from time to time so that you become personally rich as well as corporately rich.

—Tony Jeary

If you want to create true "partnerships," pay people in a way that makes them believe their expertise is valued and that they have everything to win by staying engaged with you.

10. Wealth: Be a Risk Assessor, Not a Risk Taker

> If friends and family ask for cash because you are rich,
> only give it to them as a gift. Don't expect it back.
>
> —Tony Jeary

In business deals, don't be afraid to dig deep for answers in order to assess risk. Always carry out a complete due diligence on the prospective deal, the people involved in the deal, and the finances of it.

11. Execute: Execute with Accountability!

> *Strategic Clarity* is achieved when you have a clear
> view of your vision and understand what you
> really want, why you want it, the value of doing
> it, and the highest purpose for doing it.
>
> —Tony Jeary

Though clarity, focus, and execution are strongly linked and all three are important, the most significant is execution, because execution is about doing.

12. Health (what people seem to like most): Maintain a Strong Mental Mindset

> You only get one life to live, but if you
> live it right, one life is all you need.
>
> —Peter Thomas

What goes on in your mind truly impacts your health. Assess your own self-talk daily, and your beliefs about life. Understand your outlook. Is it positive?

The book can be read front to back or used as a reference guide. Each lesson is just two pages or less, which makes it an exceptional kitchen-table read (i.e., you can read one or two principles each morning as you're having your coffee.) However you choose to read it, we hope your life will we transformed!

BOOK 41
STRATEGIC PARENTING

"Dear Daddy, you are the most incredible man I know. Thank you for all you do. You are an inspiration on how I want to live my life—enjoying my life, staying positive, and sharing the Lord in everything I do. You have been the most spectacular role model. I treasure our relationship. I love you." That note was written to me by my oldest daughter Brooke when she was 17 years old. It can't get any better than that. Our girls are a true blessing. My wife is the most wonderful mom, and together we intentionally and strategically pour into our kids.

It all started with prayer and a clear vision—a vision constantly refined by focus. Every day, and in fact virtually every hour, my wife Tammy and I determined to practice intentional effort to love, guide, protect, share, mentor, serve, model, and impact our girls until adulthood, and now beyond. I thank God daily for our blessed family and for his allowing me and Tammy to have such great parents ourselves, great mentors in our lives, great school experiences (including loving teachers and coaches), caring neighbors, and special friends.

In 1999 I had offices in China, L.A., Detroit, and Dallas; I was making millions, and yet I was having to travel sometimes more than twenty days a month all over the world. At some point during that time, I was in a hotel suite in Japan listening to Billy Graham's autobiography, *Just as I Am*. He poured out his heart in that book, and one of the things that really hit me was his big regret that he had not invested enough time with his kids. I was deeply touched that someone I admired so much and who had impacted so many people across the world would be transparent enough to say, "Here's a big mistake I made; don't make that same mistake in your life." I sat there listening to it over and over; I can remember it just like it was yesterday. His words have made a *huge* impact on my life since then, in terms of making decisions to really invest energy into my kids.

I realized I couldn't raise extraordinary kids if I was gone so much, so I decided to change my model. Although I had two offers to sell my company, I chose instead to shrink it and build a studio on my estate in Dallas and have the world's coolest high achievers come to me. A lot of people thought it wouldn't work; they said that the people who pay for advice want you come to them. I knew, though, that if I could be valuable enough, I could get special people to come to me. So I intentionally created a model where I could walk a hundred feet from my home to my studio and invest virtually every night at home with my kids. I've had the president of Walmart, the presidents of dozens of other Fortune 500 companies (like Firestone, Samsung, TGI Fridays), and other top high achievers from all over the world fly in to Dallas to invest time with me and my team in my studio. I'm extremely blessed that it works and that people keep coming back because we exceed expectations. That's our mantra. We help winners win bigger.

Fortunately, my wife and I were in sync on how to raise our kids, and we poured our lives into them. When my kids were very young, I would look for books on parenting for us to study. One book that really had an impact on me was *She Calls Me Daddy*, by Robert Wolgemuth. I looked at the kids of people who had written books on parenting to see if they were delivering exceptional kids to the world. If they were (and he did), I thought they had the right to write a book on parenting, and I had the desire to read their books.

We played out his distinction for twenty-plus years, and we've been fortunate to have two extraordinary kids. They're both serving, giving, confident, poised, world-traveled, well-liked, smart, disciplined, creative, technically savvy, and the list goes on. As I thought about how I can impact people's lives, I realized that most people aren't as strategic about raising their kids as they could be. I decided to write *Strategic Parenting* and share 100 ideas that my wife and I used to raise our two girls and attract our wonderful son-in-law.

What does the book say?

In the book you'll find 100 best practices that can dramatically impact your thinking as a parent to help you raise extraordinary kids. We encourage you to rate yourself on each one to see if you're being strategic in that area or if it may be something you need to pour more emphasis into doing. We have divided the distinctions into ten sections:

1. Set Your Kids Up to Win (Examples: expect the best of them and strategically choose the best schools)
2. Teach Your Kids That Relationships Are Everything (Examples: teach them how to serve people and guide them to choose the right friends)
3. Help Your Kids to Visualize (Examples: goal setting and family vision board)
4. Model Value for Your Kids (Examples: Be giving and grateful and do *Favors in Advance*)
5. Help Your Kids Create Their Own Brand (Examples: building their résumé, taking responsibility for what they do to create their reputation, and the advantages you get from a great personal brand)
6. Create Meaningful Family Discussions (Examples: "what did you learn" discussions and making a life, not just a living)

7. Make and Relive Memories (Examples: take lots of photos and create family video albums)
8. Provide Learning Models for Your Kids (Examples: DISC and The Five Love Languages)
9. Cool Things to Teach Your Kids (Examples: NLP and presentation skills, such as how to shake hands)
10. More Ongoing To-Do's (Examples: celebrating your kids' friends and being involved with their school)

How will the book help you?

We include an action plan at the end of the book to help you clarify your goals and dreams for your relationship with your kids and then identify specific actions to make your vision a reality. We suggest you read the book and gain ideas from the best practices we've discovered over the years, and then complete the action plan in the back of the book to help you take your relationship with your kids to a higher level.

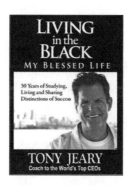

BOOK 42
LIVING IN THE BLACK
(MY AUTOBIOGRAPHY)

What are your gifts? Everyone has at least one gift; some have several. Are you using your gifts to the best of your ability?

As I neared my fiftieth birthday a few years ago, I began to reflect deeply on what I knew, what I had learned and what I believed. I wanted to build a collection of those distinctions that had been fifty years in the making. And I wanted to build it in a way that gives real value and that impacts lives—not just riches.

I teach my clients that we can and should go beyond good, beyond great, and live in *Mastery*—living in the black. In this book I use red and black as metaphors for life. "Living in the red" means aspects of your life are negative and in need of drastic improvement. Maybe your professional life is solidly in the black, and yet your home life is deeply in the red. Maybe your income is in the black, but your financial management is in the red and the stress is dragging other areas of your life down with it.

I believe you can live in *Mastery* in every area of your life—your marriage and family, your relationships, your career, and even your health—and when you do, you make living in the black a true reality.

For years I wanted to write an autobiography so my kids would have my best thinking after I'm gone. And then I wondered if anyone (besides my kids) would want to read my autobiography, since I've intentionally made my brand as a niche celebrity rather than someone who is famous to the general public.

Celebrity status in general refers to the amount of public attention given to a person by the mass media. I could build my brand to that level if I wanted to; however, I have not wanted to be so famous that people would come up to me as I'm walking down the street. My wife really prefers avoiding the public eye, so I decided not to exploit my brand to that level.

Since I'm not highly famous, I struggled for years before I wrote the book, wondering whether it would be worth the effort. Then I read Emmett Smith's book *Game On*, in which he wrote about his life in an autobiographical way, and yet the focus was on lessons he had learned through life. I thought that was a great model, so we ended up writing this book with fifty-five lessons I had learned over my lifetime.

The theme, as well as the name of the book—living in the black—stemmed from several life experiences. In 1993 I was coaching the president of Ford, and we invested one-and-a-half years planning the largest budgeted meeting ($25 million) I'd ever worked on. While the president was talking at the event, there were some forty different vehicles moving around. It was an incredible experience. As his coach, I worked with quite a few of his technical staff, and since they all wore black, I decided to wear black as well.

When I was growing up, my family owned a Standard service station. At the time, Standard had a deal with Johnny Cash. I had a standup billboard of Johnny Cash in my bedroom, left over from a Standard Oil Johnny Cash promotion, and of course he always wore black. I carried my admiration of Johnny Cash into my adult years and wanted to be like him; I also wanted to fit in when I was working with the president of Ford, and I wanted to be different. So for those myriad reasons, I decided to adopt the concept of living in the black and dressing in the black. Then, when someone hired me after seeing my picture on a book cover, I'd show up looking just like I did on the cover.

Of course, living in the black also refers to living on top of your game, and that's what this book is all about. For a few years of my life I was actually living in the red, because I wasn't necessarily aligned with my values. I was chasing money, and I went broke. I wrote the book to help people understand the powerful concept that, by constantly assessing themselves, they could live in the black instead of in the red in every area of their lives

What does the book say?

I believe that the most successful people possess a strategic mindset, and they see their lives and world differently than people who do not have that mindset. *Living in the Black* reflects a strategic approach to what I believe you may want in and for your life, which is reflected in the titles we've given to each chapter. They combine to form the acronym RESULTS, because that's the mindset I urge the reader to appropriate and develop.

Relationships: In so many ways, relationships define your life. The very core of who you are is shaped by your relationships with your parents and siblings, your friends and associates, and, most of all, with God. Great relationships can nourish your dreams, teach you true principles to live by, encourage you to grow, and help you live your life to the fullest by constantly reaching for and achieving the goals you set for yourself.

Expectations: Competition today demands more than being just good or great—it requires *Mastery*, or operating at the "living-in-the-black" level. Top leaders and achievers exceed expectations, no matter how high they are. That's why I invest so much time and energy coaching top executives, writing books, working with high-energy teams, and speaking to over-the-top groups about creating positive experiences that people would never anticipate, both professionally and personally. It takes a strong desire and an amazing support team to give more value than people expect and to have enough creativity to come up with ways to accomplish it.

Strategy: Throughout my career, I have learned that the best way to achieve extraordinary results is to become intentional about being strategic. That means acquiring new levels of discipline in terms of your thinking.

Understanding: How do you understand life? What filters, models, and principles do you use that will lead you to the "living-in-the black" level in all areas of your life? Almost every day of my life, I'm researching the distinctions of why we think the way we do and identifying principles that can affect the way we think, thus changing the total outcome of our lives.

Leverage: Leverage has probably been one of the most powerful concepts I have used to build my business and my life. For example, I leverage my marketing by using great vehicles like the Internet, magazine articles, and books that can go much farther and stay far longer than I can. I leverage my team by hiring great people who bring expertise that I don't have. I leverage my money by investing in projects that will yield far greater returns than a savings account. I leverage my resources by keeping arsenals full of valuable tools that I've collected or developed to share with others, and by tapping into the thousands of books, apps, webinars, social media networks, and other business and life tools available. The lists goes on.

Time: No one has enough time, and yet everyone has all there is. What you do with your time determines what you do with your life. In Book 4, *How to Find*

100 Extra Minutes a Day, we present my time model that basically explains that we have approximately 50 hours to invest in our business lives a week and 50 to invest in our personal lives. If we can learn to strategically manage our time well, we can win big, both professionally and personally.

Support: The greatest men and women I know—those who have achieved the level of *Mastery* in virtually every area of their lives—will all tell you that they could not have even begun the journey without the encouragement, support, and advice of the people around them. We're all part of something larger than ourselves, and we are interconnected in a way that assures our success only when we fully accept the support of others.

How will the book help you?

At the end of each chapter, you're given an assessment tool that allows you to rate where you are currently between living in the red and living in the black in the distinctions listed in that chapter. We encourage you to get the book and discover ways you can move your life up to the "living-in-the black" level in each of these powerful distinctions.

BOOK 43
LEVERAGE

If you're a leader, this book is for you. It's a spin-off of my best-selling book *Strategic Acceleration*, because in it we carefully explore further my methodology of *Clarity, Focus, and Execution*, with a huge emphasis on focus. We look at how you can get the right results faster by doing three things more often:

1. Focusing through strategic thinking
2. Focusing on *High Leverage Activities* (HLAs)
3. Reducing LLAs (*Low Leverage Activities*) by saying no more often.

When we write any book, of course, we hope it will meet its objectives. Sometimes those objectives are for the book to become a best seller, sometimes we're writing the book as a tool to share with our clients, and sometimes we write the books so we can minister to and encourage people. In fact, *Living in the Black* (Book 42) is a book I invested years in developing, and it's not even for sale; it was designed only as a gift for those I get to know.

As we publish each of our books, we don't always know which distinctions or models in the book are going to be a hit. The 3-D

Outline™ was the big hit when we wrote *Inspire Any Audience*, and *Production Before Perfection* was the most popular takeaway from *Success Acceleration*. When we wrote *Strategic Acceleration*, though, the goal was to be a best-seller from buzz factor and even create a movement where smart, aggressive people like you adopt, utilize, and rave about it to many. We knew the biggest takeaways from that book were the ability to gain clarity regarding vision and goals and focus on *High Leverage Activities* (HLAS), as well as the distinction of executing through carefully thought-out and crafted strategic communications. We were a little surprised, though, at the overwhelming popularity of the *High Leverage Activity* methodology; apparently, many people don't prioritize their lives like they should. Since the biggest takeaway from *Strategic Acceleration* ended up being HLAs, we wrote this book, *Leverage,* to specifically address that issue, with a focus on the 168-hour time model as it relates to HLAs.

What does the book say?

Gaining greater results with fewer resources is utilizing the power of leverage. In life and business the resources of time, talent, and money are always limited. Leverage those resources, and you can go faster than you ever thought, using all three for maximum gain.

Developing *High Leverage Activities* (HLAs) is an organizing principle for setting priorities. HLAs create a clarity of action, and they represent a special language that alters the way you and your team think about what needs to be done. HLAs get you the results you need faster with *less expenditure of time, money, energy, and talent.*

Establishing priorities according to leverage is some of the hardest thinking you will ever do. It's intentional thinking versus subconscious thinking.

How will the book help you?

Refer back to the 168-hour time model we included in our narrative of Book 4, *How to Gain 100 Extra Minutes a Day.* Remember that most people invest about 50 hours a week in their personal lives and 50 hours in their professional lives. This model of time links with the concept of leverage we're talking about in this book. The time you strategically invest in focusing on your *High Leverage Activities*, both personally and professionally, determines how effectively you do life.

Defining your HLAs starts by knowing where you are and where you want to go. When you determine those two pieces of information, you'll see that there's a gap between them—and that gap should be filled with the HLAs you need to focus on in order to get you where you want to go. Let me share with you both my professional and personal HLAs:

These are my HLAs on the personal side of my life:

1. Prayer
2. Investing time with my wife
3. Investing time with my family
4. Doing things that are health related, including walking, exercising, eating right, and even relaxing and counting my blessings
5. Loving people. I love to encourage and nourish the people around me. That could include writing a note to someone, sending an email, or making a phone call to my mom and loving on her.

Now here are my five professional HLAs:

1. Attracting strong, qualified business.
2. Delivering great value. Hopefully, you think that what I'm sharing with you in this *Book of Books* is powerful and that the time my team and I took to put it all together is of great value to you.
3. Clarifying the direction for TJI (our agency). That's something I own, and perhaps you own it as well for your organization, whether it's small or large. You must clarify the direction and determine how to improve and prosper the operation.
4. Gaining wisdom. What does that mean for me? I am in the wisdom business, so that means I need to constantly be sharpening my wisdom. I need to be studying, reading, and documenting my business acumen so I have a strong wisdom arsenal to share with people.

5. Nourishing my connections. I have a big Rolodex. That means I have a large number of contacts I need to nourish, so this is what I do: I autograph books every day, and I send many gifts to people. For example, last Christmas I sent out 860 personal gifts. That's because I have quite a few people I love and want to nourish. I don't want to just take from them; I want to give to them as well.

If something comes into my life that doesn't fit into one of those categories, either on the personal or professional side, I have to weigh it very carefully before I say yes to it.

My fourth professional HLA is building my wisdom arsenal, and that's why I've written fifty books. Remember, books go where you can't go and stay longer than you can stay. I was in a Bass Pro Shop not too long ago, and a guy came up to me and told me he had heard me speak at a marine dealer's group meeting. I had given him one of my books in electronic format, and he said that the book had changed his life! Now, obviously I couldn't go into this guy's home or car to mentor him and sharpen his thinking. The book did it for me! That's a pretty good leverage of time!

My commitment to giving value and exceeding expectations plays right into the concept of leveraging your time. This is especially evident when I help people turn their visions into reality in shorter time frames than they ever thought possible. And although the concept of *Elegant Solutions* originally came out in my book *Strategic Acceleration*, it obviously plays into the concept of leveraging your time, as well. (You create an *Elegant Solution* when you're so clear on what you want to accomplish that you can meet three to five objectives simultaneously through a single action.)

Leverage is the driver of results. To win, you have to get better and better at using leverage. Remember that *time* is the key differentiator in both your personal life and business. How you leverage your time will determine your results, your success, and whether or not you are winning the leadership contests.

BOOK 44
RICH RELATIONSHIPS, RICH LIFE

Why should you care about relationships? It's simple: Strong relationships help you leverage your career growth, expand your success, create your legacy (both personally and professionally), and live a happier life. Great relationships even impact the speed in which you accomplish your goals. The richer your relationships, the richer your life. Period. We at TJI are all about helping winners win more, and that includes showing you how to have great relationships.

Both my dad and my grandfather taught and demonstrated to me the principles of living happy, serving others, and cultivating strong, lifelong relationships. I'm blessed to have received such a dynamic legacy. I've lived out those principles throughout my life and career, strategically nurturing the relationships that are important to me. Every day, I live to give more value than expected to those I'm connected with, including my clients, my wife and kids, my

211

neighbors, and sometimes even strangers. How about you? Is giving value in your relationships important to you?

I'm a strong believer in the reciprocal principle (when you give to people, they will want to give back). When I help people win, they often help me win on another level. That's why I've been able to develop this profile for the type of client we want to attract, which is defined with the mnemonic ADOME:

A—Aggressive, **A**ppreciate, **A**bundance: We want clients who are aggressive in making decisions and who appreciate us and want to help us win also, because of how we've positively impacted their business and their lives. And we want clients who are not negotiating for the cheapest fee; they want us to help them build more than they have, and they'll be glad to share. They understand our track record of insuring ROI for our clients.

D—Desire to do business with us. We want people coming to us saying, "Yes, we get who you are, and we want you to help us!"

O—Open-minded. Occasionally we have people who come in with their arms folded, and I say, "Do I need to talk you into working with me? I've been doing this for thirty-something years. We have a small but one of the best and most powerful practices in the world. And if you come in open-minded, I can pour into you and your organization, and your results will take off." We want open-minded people who are ready for that.

M—Millions to be made. We prefer to work with people where there are millions of dollars at stake in terms of potential growth.

E—Equity play. We like to have the opportunity for a success fee (that is, a participation in part of the ownership or the growth of the company, based on the results we help them achieve. We will offer up less upfront fee for back-end participation, based on the results we help achieve).

I have a reciprocal relationship with the people who work for me. I'm very focused, I work harder than most people, and I probably have higher standards for my team than most others. I ask them to support my goals, and, in return, I do the same for them. I want to inspire them, encourage them, appreciate them, open doors for them, teach them, and help them learn so it will be a mutually beneficial relationship.

What does the book say?

We all have four primary types of relationships:

- Family (your parents, spouse, children, siblings, or other close relatives)
- Friends (could include your neighbors, schoolmates, co-workers, church members, or your children's friends' parents)
- Professional (typically a boss—including the board and shareholders—partners, clients, business advisors, subordinates, etc.)
- *Life Team* (may include your attorney, coach, housekeeper, plumber, groundskeeper, and any other person who helps you live life easier and smarter)

Each type of relationship can be significant to both your personal and professional life. Being strategic about each relationship and thinking through all they each bring to you can help you have a richer life. People will begin to notice that you are important to them when you are intentional, and they will want to reciprocate. Let people know they have value to you.

How will the book help you?

Do you want to have winning customers or clients who rave about you and refer others to you? Do you want to be able to lead your team in a way that makes people admire your discipline, the way you think, and the positive impact you've had on their lives? If so, this book can expand your thinking and help you and the people in your life win more, win bigger, and win with even more success.

There are seven things you can do to strategically and positively impact and grow your relationships:

1. **Ensure all stakeholders win.** This is essential, whether you're planning a charity event with multiple volunteers, managing a project with your team, or giving a sales presentation to land a new account. The more each person wins, the more vested they become in whatever the process is and the better the outcome.

2. **Understand what others want.** How do you know what they want? Ask them!

3. **Manage expectations.** If you know what people want and expect, it's much easier to make sure you meet those expectations. Here are a few best practices for managing expectations:
   ◦ **Start with knowing.** Ask people what their expectations are so there will be no mistaking or making assumptions.
   ◦ **Communicate with clarity.** Often the difference between managing expectations or not is simply clear communication.
   ◦ **Be flexible.** Be willing to adjust if someone's expectations are outside the parameters of your thinking. To strengthen and maintain relationships, be solution-oriented.

4. **Do *Favors in Advance*.** *Favors in Advance* (FIA) are favors you do for people regardless of your status with them or the desired outcome. Instead of doing favors because you expect something in return, develop an attitude of paying it forward and giving value in advance.

5. **Leverage personality styles.** Better understanding personalities (yours and those around you) can be a significant factor in the richness of your relationships. You can also often get more of what you want when you approach situations in a way that will evoke the desired response in the other person. (Refer back to Book 14, *Presenting with Style*, to learn about the DISC Personality Style Profile.)

6. **Identify your *People of Influence* (POI).** As we talked about In Book 36, *Leadership 25*, identifying the *People of Influence* in your life and then taking the time to understand what their priorities and objectives are puts you in a position to make

sure those people are winning. When you nurture your POIs and make wins for them, it will inevitably create wins for you—now or later.

7. **Have a *Partnership Mentality*.** By reframing your perspective from a "we/they" mentality to a true *Partnership Mentality* from day one, you can establish rich relationships that last for years (and even decades), experience the highest levels of success together, and nurture plenty of qualified referrals.

The more intentional you are about having fulfilling relationships, the richer and happier your life will be.

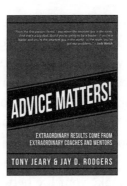

BOOK 45
ADVICE MATTERS

"If you are going to be a leader and if you're the smartest guy in the room, you've got a real problem." That quote by Jack Welch, former CEO of GE, illustrates in a powerful way why *advice matters*, which is why my co-author Jay Rogers and I chose to put it on the front cover of our book by that name.

One of the most valuable concepts I teach and live my life by is gaining clarity—doing whatever it takes to get really clear on what you want and on the best way to go about getting superior results. A great way to pinpoint the right things to do and stay on track is to seek the advice of people who can help you see life better and get more of the results you want. Do you have those kinds of people in your life?

I've been blessed all during my lifetime to have people who have poured their wisdom into me and made me who I am today. It started with my parents and grandparents, who gave me an exceptional foundation in entrepreneurship as well as life. They taught me my life's mantra—give value; do more than is expected. I've had outstanding spiritual mentors who taught me how to love God and love people better. My wife and I had three couples with exceptional daughters who were ten years older than ours support our parenting by pouring their child-rearing wisdom into us. And I've had an excellent business mentor and two coaches to whom I literally owe my success in business. Over the course of my career, they've helped me to change my thinking so I could get the remarkable results I've had. Can you think of people who have shared their wisdom, expertise, and support with you to make your life better?

I asked Jay Rodgers, my business mentor, why he invests so much of his time with me, and he said, "Because you appreciate it and you take action." I asked him what that meant, and he said, "Often when people give advice, the person they're advising doesn't take action, and you do. I appreciate that, and it makes me want to pour into you even more." I said, "Well, why don't we write a book on mentorship, then, to help others more clearly see the advantages of mentoring?"

For years, both Jay and I have poured advice and counsel into the lives of others. As you know, I've been blessed to have had the opportunities to personally advise and coach some of the world's top business leaders. Jay, on the other hand, has been a successful entrepreneur who has personally founded, grown, and sold over a dozen businesses, involving millions of net profit dollars. He has had tremendous success in his entrepreneurial projects and is past the age when most people want to kick back and retire. Yet, instead of slowing down at this stage of his life, he decided to throw his energy into founding and operating Biz Owners Ed, Inc., a nonprofit organization, for the sole purpose of mentoring serious entrepreneurs and helping them succeed. (Visit their website at www.bizownersed. com.) Together, we've helped thousands of open-minded high achievers reach levels of success that very few attain.

After we started writing the book *Advice Matters*, we decided it should be expanded beyond mentorship to include other types of advice. We came up with these six areas:
- Mentors,
- Coaches (paid mentors who have a powerful tool chest)
- Trusted colleagues

- Paid professionals (CPAs, attorneys, etc.)
- Resources (books, videos, audios, courses, etc.)
- Self (where you step back and study your own patterns and results, both good and bad)

What does the book say?

"A wise person learns from both the successes and mistakes of others." Though there are many variations of this quote, it defines a life principle that has shaped both of our lives and careers as much as any other. Since everything we do is based on the principles on our *Belief Window*, we have to constantly ensure that the principles we believe to be true are, in fact, true and up to date. We do this by studying, by intentional personal and group reflection, and by seeking outstanding advice and counsel. The right advisors will help us make the right choices based on accurate and current information.

We all have *Blind Spots*— things on our *Belief Windows* that we can't see unless uncovered by something or someone else. In order to move through life better, you need to get advice that will help you uncover your *Blind Spots* and change your *Belief Window.*

How will the book help you?

There are four simple steps to help you navigate through the choices and options available for getting advice:

1. Identify your issues and opportunities. Look at where you are compared to where you want to be, and list the issues you're struggling with that are keeping you from crossing that gap. Make a list of the opportunities available to you, as well, so you can seek wisdom and input as to how (or whether) to move forward.

2. Determine the best resource(s) to go after to get your advice from. You may want to start with trusted colleagues and a mentor or two until your revenue can support a coach. Consider that the right coach can steer you in the best direction, help you avoid catastrophic mistakes, and often give advice that brings in a huge payoff. Or your situation

may call for choosing one or more paid advisors you can trust and who can give you master advice. And also remember all of the resources (books, videos, URLs, etc.) available to you. Consider investing as much time as you can studying as many resources as you can to learn as much as you can. And finally, be sure to devote time reflecting on your past experiences and learning from yourself.

3. Gather options or possible solutions from your advisor(s), and then review the plusses and minuses (including the risks). The buck stops with you. Listen to the suggestions served up by your coach, your mentor(s), your trusted colleagues, and/or your paid advisors; and list any ideas or options you identified from your resources and self-reflection. Then carefully weigh all of the information and options you've gathered.

4. Take action accordingly. After careful consideration of all of your options, confidently choose the best path for you and go forward based on the advice of what, where, why, how, and when you received from your advisors.

As you're choosing your advisors, there are five very important criteria to look for:

1. Do they have the proven track record and real-life experience to lead you where you want to go?

2. Do they have the personal success and expertise to qualify their advice?

3. Do they have an extensive arsenal of tools to help you learn and leverage your time?

4. How many connections do they have (Rolodex), and are they willing to share their connections with you and open doors?

5. Do their values match yours?

Advice matters. This wise verse from Proverbs 11:14 says it all: "Where there is no counsel, the people fall: but in the multitude of counselors there is safety" (New King James Version).

BOOK 46
STRATEGIC SELLING

My theme, "Be intentionally strategic in everything you do," is especially powerful in the area of selling. Virtually every company in existence wants growth, and that entails branding, marketing, and selling. At TJI, we reinforce a strategic and well-thought-out relationship among all three, and we've published books, whitepapers, and articles on each of these very important subjects.

In today's fast and ever-changing world, the importance of setting yourself up for extraordinary results is absolutely critical to winning. You may be a salesperson, a sales manager, an organizational leader, or an individual who just wants to become more exceptional at presenting your ideas in a way that gets people to take action. Wherever you fit in that mix, this unique book will equip you with decades of my study on this subject as we reveal twenty-five of the proven best practices I teach my clients.

For years, our organization has worked with the world's top leaders and companies. Our organization helped turn around Chrysler in the early '90s, was commissioned to redevelop Walmart's training in the late '90s, and helped triple Firestone's non-tire business in the early 2000s. In the time since then, we've advised the presidents of NY Life, Samsung, and TGI Fridays, among others. Working with and coaching these and other influential clients, I have developed a training model based on these four basic components, and in the book we cover all four.

1. Awareness (help people become aware of what they don't see)
2. Skills (sharpen skillsets)
3. Processes (build and improve the steps, and put them to use)
4. Tools (the right tools give leverage)

Based on the best practices offered in this book, I also developed a concept a few years ago called Pitch Mastery™, which helps you present your methodology, your offerings, your products, and your services.

What does the book say?

There are ten steps to the Pitch Mastery™ methodology, which cover all four of the basic components of the *Strategic Selling* training model:

Awareness:

1. Develop an opportunity and overview timeline to define the whole picture.
2. Create a matrix of the client players to define the people involved.

Skills:

3. Create a team matrix to define the team that will help the client win.
4. Develop a presentation matrix that will enable you to grasp all the presentation opportunities.

Processes:

5. Prepare a 3-D Outline™ to ensure clarity of each presentation.

Tools:

6. Create a tools matrix that lists all the tools you need to build for your presentation.
7. Develop a "tough questions" matrix to help you identify answers to potential objects and enhance your confidence.
8. Prepare an influence matrix to help you strategically improve your influence.
9. Create a "What If's" matrix to help you gain more confidence and prepare for possibilities.
10. Create a debrief matrix to ensure continuous learning.

Closing business effectively is critical to your and your organization's overall success. We encourage you to be strategic about your sales efforts so you can create more predictable wins.

BOOK 47
CHANGE
MINDSET MATTERS

Often when I'm speaking to large groups, I'll ask people to raise their hands if they need help with change in any area of their lives. Usually almost everyone in the room raises their hand. How about you? Is there an area of your life where you would like to see some change?

According to research, 30 percent of people hate change, 50 percent are in the middle (they may think "this too shall pass or that it doesn't apply to them), and only 20 percent fully embrace change. What that means is, every time you try to effect change in an organization, you initially only have the full support of 20 percent of the people!

It's all about managing mindset. You may remember that in 1991 I was commissioned to be part of a team to help Chrysler become the best company in the world. The company leaders knew that the best way to do that was to change the customer experience, so we were commissioned to help write and lead Customer One, which *changed the way dealers and distributors looked at customer service (changed their mindset)*. We hired consultants to go around the world and challenge the way dealers thought, and we used self-discovery to initiate the change by having the consultants ask the dealers, "Do you see a need to change?" Of course they all did, so it opened their minds to solutions that would change their current outcomes, which ultimately led to Chrysler's extraordinary turnaround. It was all just a matter of changing their mindset.

What does the book say?

Without change, there is no innovation, creativity, or incentive for improvement. People come up with many reasons to resist change, and yet change can be a beautiful thing. The most successful people embrace it and have a positive, solution-oriented mindset that focuses on possibilities. They know how to manage change effectively because they know a secret: mindset matters.

This book was developed to help both individuals and leaders of organizations manage change well. There are four pieces to the change puzzle:

1. Life: It is always changing.
2. Individual: Each person will either be resistant or indifferent or will embrace change.
3. Leadership: Leaders have vision (hope) for the future and strategically share it.
4. Organizational: The culture of your organization impacts success.

How will the book help you?

What is your organizational culture? Does it foster change and working together as a *High-Performing Team*?

I invested months studying, dissecting, and understanding top cultures and developing distinctions of true team building. In the process, I found that companies and even departments operate in one of three camps:

1. Group: A group is people working together with no clear common vision or goal; there's not much synergy, and each person or department executes independently.
2. Team: A team will typically work together with more synergy; they are a group of people working together for a common goal and are interdependent.
3. *High Performing Team* (HPT): A *High Performing Team* is a synergized team that focuses on being as effective as possible while continually reevaluating to work toward quality processes. Each team member is individually motivated and has a high level of investment in accomplishing the goal.

To create a culture focused on *High Performing Teams*, there are three foundations that greatly contribute to its success (remember ACT):

1. **A**ccountability: Do what you say you're going to do, when or before you said you'd do it.
2. **C**ommunication: Have a plan and communicate. Having a plan and communicating that plan will not only support proper execution; it will also alleviate questions and reservations your team may have about the process.
3. **T**rust: Trust is so important for any organizational effort, and team members need to be able to rely on one another as well as their leadership.

Remember the *Belief Window* and paradigm "sister" concepts we talked about in Book 10, *Success Acceleration*? My friend and client Joel Barker made the word "paradigm" a household word when he wrote the book *Paradigms: The Business of Discovering the Future*, and developed the accompanying video called "The Business of Paradigms." Whether you use the terms *Belief Window*, paradigm, or changing mindsets, they all refer to the principle that success only comes to those who strategically think in a way that leads to the very best outcomes. Mindset matters.

BOOK 48
RESULTS FASTER!

What does a bullseye represent to you? When you're able to hit the bullseye right in the center of a target, it means you've hit the highest level of success! Right? You know you've hit the mark and achieved the results you're looking for. We chose the bullseye as a visual model to represent this book because the book contains twenty-one of my most powerful lessons that have helped top leaders all over the world hit the bullseye and achieve extraordinary results.

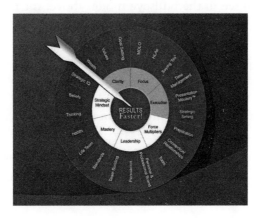

I've been coaching my good friend Stuart Johnson, the owner of *SUCCESS* magazine, for years, and a couple of years ago he decided to create a series of online video courses for his SUCCESS Academy featuring the best work of world-known authors and authorities. Stewart asked me to be one of his featured experts. As we were planning my video course, we decided to name it RESULTS Faster! because many of the world's top achievers come to me to get . . . well . . . the best results faster.

Stewart hired Pam Hendrickson, who was the top IP expert on Tony Robbins' team for eighteen years. Pam collaborated with both the SUCCESS team and my team to extract the best out of the forty-four books I had written up to that point. The video course turned out exceptionally well; it gives my very best thinking from my entire life's study on how you can get the right results you want faster.

After we finished the video course, we decided to write the companion book by the same name. I consider this book the crown jewel of all my books so far, because it encapsulates twenty-one of my very best teachings

What does the book say?

The RESULTS Faster! digital course, and ultimately the book, gives you access to the tools, skills, and techniques utilized by our clients—top companies, CEOs, and super achievers who embrace my revolutionary "more-results-in-less-time" approach to goal achievement. (Visit tonyjeary.com/resultsfasterwebinar for more information on how to access the course.)

As you can see in the bullseye model above, the twenty-one lessons are divided into seven clear areas, which we've listed out below:

Strategic Mindset

1. Thinking: Change your thinking, change your results.
2. Beliefs: Ensure the principles on your window are true and accurate.
3. Strategic IQ: Not only should you balance tactical and strategic, but you should also be intentionally strategic about everything if you want the right results faster.

Clarity

4. Wealth: We all want it, and it's a lot more than money; live on purpose and spend time doing what makes you happy and/or what you are really passionate about.

5. Values: Whether it's a business or just you, a must is to have clearly defined values and make sure you have alignment with your goals.

6. Goal Setting: Goals need to be written, visualized, and mentally owned . . . and then you can actually *Design Your Own Life*.

Focus

7. MOLO: Know what you want more of and less of and what you should do more of and less of.

8. HLA's: *High Leverage Activities* (HLAs) should help you filter, both personally and professionally.

9. Saying No: Saying no smartly has a big payoff. With both MOLO and HLAs defined, combined with strong discipline, you can more easily avoid *Low Leverage Activities* (LLAs).

Execution

10. Time: Where and how you invest your time and energy will determine your results ... period!

11. Presentation Mastery™: *Life Is a Series of Presentations*. In fact, life is also a series of persuasions.

12. Strategic Selling: Being strategic versus just being skillful can greatly impact the results you get.

Force Multipliers

13. Preparation: Prepare, prepare, prepare!

14. Connections/Relationships: It really is about who you know when you want to make it happen faster.

15. Tools (tool chest): Tools work! The stronger your tool chest (arsenal), the faster and more impactful you will be.

Leadership

16. Professional Brand: Your strategic presence, or your brand, has a huge impact on how people follow your lead.
17. Persuasion: Extraordinary leadership must include influencing people to take action.
18. Team Building: There are three magic keys to building exceptional teams: accountability, communication, and trust.

Mastery

19. Standards: Set up a list of standards, both personal and professional, and live them.
20. *Life Team*: *Life Team* members help you extend your ability to get things done, make better decisions, and do more of what you love.
21. Habits: Acquire pattern(s) of behavior that often lead to the proven outcomes you desire.

Notice that we started the book with *Strategic Mindset*—thinking. That's the main theme we've emphasized over and over in this *Book of Books*, because that's where it all starts if you want extraordinary results.

What will the book do for you?

The heart of the book is the three-step *Strategic Acceleration* "magic formula" I've developed and proven out over and over through the years—*Clarity, Focus, and Execution*—for quickly getting the exact results you want by pulling all the right pieces together.

By living out the twenty-one powerful lessons in this book, you can dramatically impact your success and get the right RESULTS Faster!

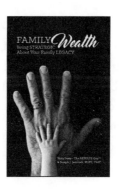

BOOK 49
FAMILY WEALTH

We all have a legacy, and yet many of us fail to intentionally and strategically plan what our legacy will be, especially as it pertains to our families. Is your legacy important to you? Do you know (with clarity) what you will be passing down in terms of legacy to your children, your grandchildren, and even beyond? Are you taking the steps now to ensure your legacy plays out the way you want?

We hope everything you've done—building a successful life and meaningful fortune, persevering through great challenges and opportunities, and making the world a better place—will continue when you're gone from this world. Isn't that what you want, as well?

When I started coaching Joseph Janiczek, the founder and owner of Janiczek Wealth Management, there was an instant connection. We both realized that our individual visions and life's work shared much common ground, especially when it came to helping other people build a legacy for their families. This book is the result of our collaboration.

What does the book say?

This book continues with my life's theme of being intentionally strategic about everything you do. It's a tool that we hope will open your mind to the idea of being strategic about how you want to pass on your wealth to the following generations. And by wealth, we mean much more than just money. Wealth, under our definition, includes:

- Monetary items, such as:
  - Investments
  - Companies
  - Interests
- Nonmonetary items, such as:
  - Wisdom (including thinking, principles, and standards
  - Reputation/brand
  - Contacts (business contacts and your *Life Team*)
  - Intellectual property
  - Philanthropy
  - Methodology
  - Capabilities (including skills, knowledge, processes, and systems)
  - Spiritual understanding and formation
  - Mindsets
  - Values
  - Work ethics
  - Beliefs
- Other desirable advantages, such as:
  - High level of confidence
  - Trust
  - Self-esteem
  - Humility
  - Connections
  - Commitments
  - Habits

Families who see financial resources as only one part of an abundant life are more likely to pinpoint and transmit essential, life-enhancing value and wisdom over time and successfully pass down their all-encompassing wealth.

How will the book help you?

We've included an overview of the book below.

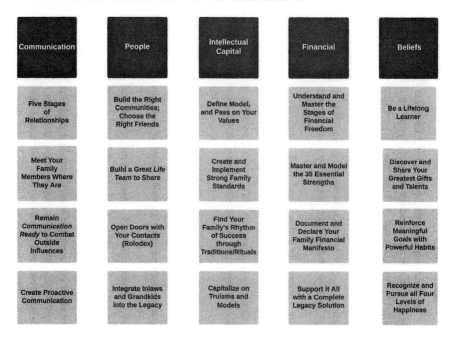

As you can see, the book is content-rich. We suspect much of what we present in the book will be new to you, as we've included many well-thought-out and proven best practices to help you crystalize your thoughts and ideas about your family legacy. We hope you will be inspired to intentionally and strategically formulate your plan and start acting on it now so it can benefit you and your family.

BOOK 50
LIVING LIFE SMILING

How do you define happiness? What brings you true joy and fulfillment in life?

My good friend Daryl Homes is founder and managing director of 1300SMILES, a dental group in Australia. He and I have both studied happiness for many years, and we have discovered that there are certain things that can greatly contribute to living a happy and joyful life. Our research, along with our own life experiences, has shown us that happiness is a choice that people elect to bring into their lives despite their circumstances.

This book is actually an extension of my continued fascination with the distinctions that lead to living a happy and successful life. I first wrote the precursor to his book, *A Good Sense Guide to Happiness*, in 1999. I had become intrigued with the whole idea of the difference between joy and happiness and started studying the concept of happiness to the point that I became somewhat of an expert on the subject.

This book was birthed in front of a fire during a shared ski trip in Colorado, as Daryl and I discussed all there is in life to be truly thankful for. We both understand that genuinely appreciating those things is what helps us to personally live life smiling. And because we believe that helping others be truly happy in life is one of the most significant things we can do, we share in the book things that have been important in creating happiness in our own lives.

What does the book say?

We explore six key areas that are critical to finding and living a life of happiness, which together form the acronym SMILES:

Significance:	Doing what is most meaningful and what matters the most
Money:	Enjoying cash flow, financial freedom, and being positioned to help others
Inspiration:	Having positive emotions and a motivated state of mind
Lifestyle:	Living a life that includes intentionally creating good habits and actions
Engagement:	Being immersed in work and the people you love and enjoy
SUCCESS:	Living with purpose and alignment, and ensuring others win!

How will the book help you?

Before reading the book to dig deeper into how to cultivate even more happiness, use the *Happiness Index* below to examine your current state. Rate your current level of happiness within each of the six areas from 1–20 (with 20 being the highest). Then total your score to find your starting point.

Happiness Index

What	Description	Score
Significance	*You do what matters most to you.* You have alignment of values, and you have clearly defined your purpose and live this purpose intentionally and fully. You have self-acceptance, you focus on your unique strengths, and you have a strong sense of inner peace.	
Money	*You have cash flow, reserves, financial security, and financial freedom, and you do valuable things for others.* You have acquired wealth, are content with your circumstances, and have a satisfying net worth. You give back to others and have a sense of security.	
Inspiration	*You have positive emotions and are energized. You have a high level of self-motivation.* You are generally an optimistic person and create experiences regularly that inspire you. You have a great sense of self-worth and enjoy the small things as well as the big things.	

(Continued)

What	Description	Score
Lifestyle	*You put habits into place that support the lifestyle you want.* You are patient (yet persistent) in going after your goals. You place a high degree of importance on your health in the form of diet, exercise, and a positive mental mindset. You value creating a home versus having a house, and you genuinely enjoy the journey of your life.	
Engagement	*You become immersed in your work, the people you love, your friendships, and your leisure.* You have great, balanced relationships. You surround yourself with positive people and eliminate toxic ones. You have a solid *Life Team* supporting you. You have a healthy respect for yourself, others, and authority.	
Success	*You live a happy, fulfilled life with purpose and alignment, and you ensure that others win!* You are excited about what you're doing, sticking to what matters during tough times, and living a life you can be proud of and that others will want to share with you.	Total Score:

Being happy is the greatest gift you can give yourself. It's a conscious choice. Though there will be bad days along the way, by choosing to be grateful for the things you have and intentionally working toward the things you want, you can have the life of your dreams—one that is created uniquely for you, by you.

CONCLUSION

As I mentioned in the introduction, my president and coach for twenty years, Jim Norman, and I started writing a special book that would have made it into my first fifty had Jim not passed away before we were able to complete it. The book, called *Thinking: Change Your Thinking, Change Your Results*, would have been phenomenal.

In prior years, because of Jim's influence, I had become even more fascinated with the topic of thinking, and he and I agreed to co-author a powerful book on the subject. The book was to include how he had helped both Zig Ziglar, as president of his company, and me, as my president, think differently. More importantly, though, we wanted the book to expand the reader's understanding of the topic of thinking as it relates to extraordinary achievement of results. We knew if we could influence people to change their thinking and become intentionally strategic about everything they did, they could see greater results in every area of their lives.

We were able to complete chapter one before Jim passed away, and my team and I decided to share it with you here. Now that you've read this *Book of Books*, you can see that strategic thinking is the foundation of everything I now teach and all the books I now write. Even the best takeaways from my earlier books reflected that theme, before Jim helped me understand in 2006 that helping people think was my strong suit.

Please enjoy this first chapter of *Thinking,* in honor of Jim, the greatest thinker I've ever met.

CHAPTER ONE

THINKING
CHANGE YOUR THINKING,
CHANGE YOUR RESULTS

The Pursuit of Mastery

Tony Jeary: I began to study personal development when I was sixteen years old. For some reason I had an insatiable desire to learn more, and I felt compelled to help others do the same. This passion for personal growth allowed me to quickly adapt when I became an adult and stepped into the business world as an entrepreneur. I have built an extraordinary business strategizing for the leaders of some of the most successful organizations in the world, as well as high-performing individuals and entrepreneurs. The simple explanation for my success is that I help people positively change their thinking and their results. In fact, I encourage, guide, and help them achieve superior results faster as they begin to think differently.

Until a few years ago I knew thinking was important, and yet I didn't see it as the foundational issue for achieving results. One day my coach and president Jim Norman said something to me that started me down the road of learning more and more about thinking, which has led to the writing of this book. Jim said, "You know, Tony, thinking is hard." I had never thought about thinking being hard. What Jim meant, of course, was that thinking properly, in a focused way that has measurable value, is hard.

In the years that followed, Jim and I collaborated and developed the *Strategic Acceleration* methodology that has become the foundation of all I do today. My book *Strategic Acceleration* was published in 2009, and its core concepts involve three simple words: Clarity, Focus, and Execution. The teaching, tools, and suggestions found in the book actually provide the blueprint for developing a focused thinking plan, even though the primary message of the book was not about thought change. Rather, I provided practical tools and solutions for accelerated results without really dealing with the foundational cause—thinking—in depth.

Since that book was published, the issue of focused thinking has become so important in what I teach that the decision to write this book was easy. So you could say this book is the companion book to *Strategic Acceleration*. It explains why the concepts in *Strategic Acceleration* work so powerfully for the people who choose to deploy its tools and principles.

I have much more to say about thinking and results; however, before I get into more detail, I have a question for you to consider: What kind of person are you?

Are you the kind of person who hopes to perform at a peak level, who wants to get the most out of life, and who wants to continually raise the bar of your performance? If so, it's fair to say that you're probably very interested in the results you get from your effort. Several years ago, I created a term called *Return on Effort* (ROE). ROE is about getting the best possible results from the most compressed amount of time and energy invested. Consistently achieving a high ROE also involves the pursuit of not only *great* results, but *extraordinary* results. I'm talking about the kind of results that are eye-popping, the kind of results that you may have previously thought impossible to achieve.

I teach that there is a progression of satisfactory results involving three stages. Most people and organizations are satisfied with *good* results. Then a smaller percentage of people want to accelerate their results and perform at a level of *greatness.* The third stage is one I call *Mastery.* Most of my newer customers are those who are performing at the great level, and yet they have a burning desire to do more. They want to perform at the *Mastery* level. The shift to *Mastery* involves a specific change in thinking; then the principles of *Strategic Acceleration* must be executed to translate their new thinking into action, and ultimately to superior results!

What do you think of when you hear the word *Mastery*? Most people think in terms of being elite or being the best they can be.

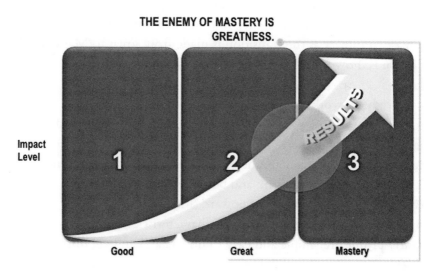

THE ENEMY OF MASTERY IS GREATNESS.

Impact Level

1   2   3

Good   Great   Mastery

While those ideas are accurate, to me *Mastery* involves much more. To illustrate, let me share with you what I call the impact curve.

We've talked about the three possibilities when it comes to acceptable results. The first possibility is "good," and that's where most successful businesses operate. "Good" companies are profitable, and they experience some growth. They have developed business practices that work for them, and they stick to them. They are typically conservative when it comes to change, and their innovation level is about average. Organizations in this category are satisfied with who and what they are. They have settled into a comfort zone and rarely take any action to disrupt it.

The second possibility is "great." "Great" businesses are "good" companies that dared to do some things differently. They have developed the ability to think more strategically, and they have combined strategic thinking with the focus needed to create the strategies that propelled them to greater success. When a business or a person achieves "greatness," they have difficulty grasping that there is yet a third possibility that awaits them. Their problem is that they believe they have already achieved as much as possible. At that point, their greatness becomes a silent enemy and a roadblock to discovering the third possibility of achievement: *Mastery*.

To achieve *Mastery*, there must be a shift in thinking that is very specific, and this applies to both individuals and organizations. If we revisit the impact curve graphic, you can see how there is a huge increase in impact as the transition is made from great to Mastery. The question is, how is that dramatic change ignited and what does it look like?

I've been working with top performing individuals and organizations for the past twenty-five years and have identified a very specific profile of *Mastery*. There are five essential characteristics of Mastery, and all of them are the result of a specific way of thinking. As individuals begin to think and believe some specific new principles, there is a consistent upward shift in superior results on the impact curve. The five foundational characteristics that produce the *Mastery* profile are simple and easy to understand and yet difficult to achieve.

The Five Characteristics of Mastery

These five foundational characteristics of Mastery produce an action profile that is consistent for both individuals and organizations.

1. There is a *compelling strategic vision* and a deep motivation to achieve it. Clarity exists about why the vision must be achieved, as well as its value and significance.
2. There is a *desire to achieve perfection*. Perfection is understood to be about *always* doing the right things at the right time and making no mistakes.
3. There is an *obsession to learn*, grow, and improve.
4. There is an *ability to think on a long-term basis* and focus on outcomes and vision execution.
5. There is a consistent ability to convert *challenges into opportunities*.

Jim Norman: I became fascinated with the issue of thinking over thirty years ago, when I was struggling with some issues of personal and professional change and discovering how difficult authentic change was. I eventually learned that when I changed my thinking, it became possible to easily change my behavior and actions, which then changed my results. However, I also learned that learning to think differently was hard.

This year I will be 72 years old. My business career has been divided into three phases. Phase one lasted twenty years, and I was an entrepreneur. I started, built, and sold three successful businesses. In phase two, I became the president and CEO of the legendary motivator Zig Ziglar's company. Ziglar was my father-in-law, and I took on this position at the request of Zig and our family. I worked with Zig for six years. Phase three began after I left Ziglar. I became an executive coach and a strategy/branding consultant. My first customer after leaving Ziglar was Tony Jeary, and that was in 1996. Tony and I have been collaborating ever since.

Tony Jeary is hands-down the most focused and self-disciplined human being I have ever known. And yet the most remarkable fact about Tony is his ability to work with others and facilitate great positive transformation in their businesses and in their personal lives. He has worked with some of the largest companies in the world and some of the greatest entrepreneurs. How has Tony achieved so much? Well, he has the ability to help people change some things they believe about themselves and their businesses and then create action plans of impact that are practical, executable, and focused. He helps them achieve great clarity about what they really want. He helps them develop a level of focus they have never experienced concerning what really matters and what it takes to produce superior results. Then he helps them develop action strategies and tools to execute them in a powerful way. The magic is that he can accomplish all this quickly. Typically, in a one-day session with the top leaders of organizations, he is able to ignite a spark of change that puts them on a new path of success and results. You might think this is impossible, and yet I have been watching Tony do this for almost twenty years.

You Become What You Think

I mentioned that I became fascinated with change and the relationship of thinking to change in the '80s. In the '90s, as the CEO of Zig Ziglar's business, I was fortunate to have a ringside seat with a man who did so much to encourage millions of people around the world to higher levels of success. Zig Ziglar understood the power of thinking, and it formed the bedrock of all he taught about success and achievement.

It is a fact that the great motivational speakers of history have all based their teaching for producing individual change on helping people change what they think and believe about themselves and others. Zig Ziglar possibly said it best: "You can change who you are and what you are by changing what goes into your mind." Ziglar got the action part correct, and yet he stopped short of explaining why and how this works or how this principle can be applied to creating and executing leadership strategies. Any leader who hopes to produce mastery in their organization must understand how this works and understand thought change as a leadership tool by design.

Usually you will find two kinds of people in every organization. There are the "enterprise" thinkers, and there are the "dependent" thinkers. Enterprise thinkers are the people who work tirelessly to achieve and succeed. They believe in themselves, and they push the envelopes of success. Enterprise thinkers usually make up the leadership team and those who will eventually become leaders. Dependent thinkers rarely come up with any new ideas for better results; they are dependent on others to do that. They wait to be told what they need to do next. They love the status quo and are comfortable in it. They actually resist any change they perceive might disrupt or threaten their comfort zone. Dependent thinkers always have many reasons to avoid doing anything new.

Enterprise thinkers are usually a minority and are outnumbered by the dependent thinkers. So when it comes to change and improvement, it's easy to see that an organizational thought war will be the most difficult part of creating the change. Enterprise thinkers will embrace the change when they believe in the strategy for change. Dependent thinkers will resist! What kind of person are you—an enterprise thinker or a dependent thinker? Or are you a little of both? It's very easy to believe yourself to be an enterprise thinker and yet function in behavior as a dependent thinker.

In 1922 Henry Ford published a book entitled *My Life and Work*. One of his major themes was his admiration for Thomas Edison and the importance of thinking. Ford suggested that everyone needs to continually refine their "thinking power." He also observed that most people chose jobs that enabled them to not have to think. His admiration for Edison was based on the inventor's ability to "think things through." Clearly, in Ford's opinion, Edison was an enterprise thinker, and most other people were dependent thinkers.

The relevance of enterprise and dependent thinking in organizations relates to problem solving. When you experience results that are less than hoped for or possibly even a serious failing that actually threatens the organization's survival, the first question that raises its head is *why*? Why did this happen? Then, *how* did it happen? Eventually, these questions blur into blame, and the people responsible are identified and disciplined in a variety of ways. After there is some sort of agreement as to how, why, and who, the quest for solutions and corrections begin. It's then that many different solutions to problem solving are considered and deployed. If everyone involved in the problem-solving process could agree on a common truth about the origin of problems, the problem-solving process would be easier and faster.

Is there a common element to all problems, regardless of the nature of the problem? I believe there is, and the common element is thinking! Every new project, strategy, or activity first appeared in someone's mind as an idea. That means thought is the most basic element in creating, planning, and executing any strategy. It also means that errors in thinking are the root cause of a failed or disappointing strategy. So thinking is the common element for analyzing poor results. Based on that concept, flawed thinking becomes the real problem. To correct any failure, the process requires identification of the flawed thinking and some analysis as to why the thinking was flawed. What was believed to be true that wasn't true? That question will always reveal that something believed to be true was not true, and that's the reason the strategy failed.

Enterprise thinkers are more likely to properly identify the thinking causes of failure than dependent thinkers. Dependent thinkers will be more comfortable trying to do the same things over again hoping for a different result. Their motive to stay in their comfort zone is stronger than their desire to find better solutions. Enterprise thinkers will be willing to take greater risks, even at the risk of threatening comfort zones. The leadership challenge is to reconcile these types of thinking, develop a new strategy based on some new thinking, and deploy that strategy throughout the organization's culture.

It's now easy to see why thinking is the root cause of success and failure. It's also easy to see why Tony Jeary is so successful in helping to transform organizations from great to *Mastery*. He begins solving problems at the level of thought change that flows into new strategies. He helps people and organizations develop new cultures based on new thinking that embraces the Five Foundational Characteristics of Mastery!

Tony Jeary: Today, most people really don't care that much about doing the hard work required to function at the level of greatness or *Mastery*. Most people prefer creating a comfort zone around themselves and maintaining it. For those with this kind of mindset, apathy rules and any meaningful change is a possible threat.

The thing about thought that drives opinion and ultimately action is belief. The things you believe to be true are your mental constitution, and it is very difficult to think and accept ideas that conflict with what you believe to be true. Essentially, it's the things you believe to be true (about everything) that make you different from everyone else. The truth you embrace shapes your opinions, your personality, and most visibly the things you actually do. The things you do communicate who and what you are to others, and what you do is driven by what you believe.

So if you want to change what you do in order to achieve a better result, you must ultimately change what you believe about something. It's only when you change what you believe that you can change the way you think. When you change the way you think, you can make better choices. When you make better choices, you can achieve better results! When you continually improve your results, you eventually transition from good to great to *Mastery*.

Thinking has always been important, and yet it's never been as important as it is today. The sheer volume and speed of information retrieval has complicated the ability to achieve great results. Why? It's because of the incredible volume of information so easily discoverable and available. It can be both overwhelming and distracting. When you're distracted, your thinking is not focused, and the effort you expend is defused. This means your ROE is lower than it could have been. The antidote for unfocused thought and defused effort is strategic thinking—the ability to process information and filter it by relevance to the overall vision and your most important goals. The ability to think strategically will generate the highest degree of leverage for your effort! It is also the ability that will eventually elevate your results from great to *Mastery*.

Strategic thinking can best be understood as the kind of thinking that focuses on execution of a vision, winning, and creating a competitive advantage. Strategic thinking gives you the ability to identify and wrap yourself around the things that really matter. Strategic thinking makes it possible for you to "see" the final vision and all the major action steps that must be taken to transport you from where you are today to your ultimate vision of the future. It is through this kind of thinking that wars are won, sports teams and individuals become champions, and businesses dominate market share.

Problem Solving

In the shift from great to *Mastery*, many decisions have to be made that are related to problem solving. Since a major component of *Mastery* is a desire for perfection, it is necessary to critically evaluate a great many decisions, priorities, and strategies. The evaluation involves using problem-solving skills with a new mindset. Albert Einstein wisely said, *"We cannot solve our problems with the same thinking we used when we created them."* It is significant to note that Einstein is clearly saying that *problems are caused by thinking.* Here is another familiar pop-culture saying: "Doing the same things over and over again and expecting different results is a form of insanity." Both Einstein's remark and that truism clearly imply that if you want to change your results, you have to change your thinking.

Leaders and top performers come to my *Strategic Acceleration* studio for essentially one reason: They have come up against a results barrier that they can't seem to break through and overcome. They want to achieve a higher level of performance, and they have exhausted their own methods. They face problems that block them, and they know they must overcome those problems if they hope to achieve better results and increase their ROE. My experience proves that Einstein was correct—every problem or challenge can be traced to a thinking problem, and the thinking that produced the less-than-expected results must be identified and changed.

When you confront problems, you can make the problem-solving process simple, or you can make it very complicated. Since every problem can be traced back to flawed thinking, the challenge to solve the problem involves the mind. The essential problem is making the mind obedient to the truth it needs to accept to correct the problem. The challenge for organizations is that many minds within the organization must become obedient to the truth that must be accepted.

There are four stages of mental change required for a problem-solving breakthrough:

Stage One: Recognize denial. When problems are confronted, the common human response is denial and excuse making. Denial can only be overcome by taking responsibility for the problem and being honest about it. This can be a threatening process for many, and can be strongly resisted.

Stage Two: Acceptance. People must take responsibility for causes of the problem.

Stage Three: Identify the truth that needs to be accepted. This stage requires that people identify the thinking that must be deployed to remedy the problem.

Stage Four: Execute a new strategy. Based on the new thinking, a new strategy must be created and executed.

★★★★★

The balance of this book would have provided a more detailed look at not only the problem-solving process, but would have also explained how to create the Five Characteristics of Mastery in your own life or in your organization.

I hope the takeaways from my fifty books in this *Book of Books* and the first chapter of the book *Thinking* that Jim and I wrote together have reinforced the importance of being strategic about everything in life, both personally and professionally. A major component of being strategic, of course, is thinking. The better you think, the more strategic you can be; and the more strategic you are, the more valuable you are to yourself, to your family, to your vocation, and to the world. Every problem you encounter is a thinking problem, so every problem can be solved by changing your thinking. Learning to think strategically can dramatically increase your *Return on Effort* (ROE) and produce extraordinary results. Jim was right: Thinking *is* hard, and yet the results are so worth it!

Because we truly believe in the life-changing power of books, and we know that books can go where we can't go and stay longer than we can stay, we've already started on our next fifty. In fact, in the queue to be published soon are:

Strategic Eating: You can and should be strategic about everything that matters, and that includes the food you eat. My co-author Jenn Lewis and I have listed out twenty-five healthy eating strategies you must know, understand, do, and form habits around.

Becoming a Strategic Networker: Ryan Chamberlin and I merged our expertise—his as one of the top networkers in the MLM industry and mine as a strategist to some of the top business leaders in the world—to bring you the seven results principles for building a massive networking organization.

The Science of Goal Achievement: I collaborated with my late friend Dr. Kevin Light, a cosmetic surgeon and expert in integrative medicine, to bring you astonishing ways the brain, the mind, and the body work together to support goal achievement.

Black Card Access: Having traveled extensively throughout my career, I've learned a host of travel secrets. I share many of them with you in this book and teach you how to strategically travel better and live in style.

Tony Jeary on Wisdom: It's all about thinking, and thinking is limited by your vocabulary, experiences, teachings, and focus. Wisdom allows for better decisions, and better decisions equal better results. You need wisdom in your personal life, and you need it for your team, large or small (i.e., the collective wisdom of your team, your department, your organization, or even your whole company). Wisdom—grow it, use it, accumulate it, and of course bring it into your team.

The Healthy 100: Dr. Gerry Edelman, a leading oncologist in the Dallas area, teamed up with me to bust health myths and deliver 100 things you should know to understand the way the brain, the mind, and the body work to support your goal achievement.

Money Mastery: My master money-making long-time friend Jack Furst and I came together to create a powerful book that guides you through the process of wealth creation. Starting with working smartly and spending less than you make, which creates a *Surplus*, we give you smart distinctions about saving and then investing wisely, which eventually leads you to wealth creation.

The Momentum Factor: My second book with Jack Furst combines my *Clarity, Focus and Execution* methodology with our 9 P Model—passion, purpose, provision, people, priorities, programs, plans, performance, and profit—and focuses on the more tactical side of the methodology.

Tony Jeary's Top Models: I believe one of the fastest ways to learn anything is through models, and I've used models as a primary teaching tool throughout my thirty years of helping people get extraordinary results. I've collected many of the best and created many of my own to supplement the distinctions I teach.

God has blessed me beyond belief. He's given me favor to positively impact people's lives and businesses. I don't take that favor lightly. I plan to take the next fifty-plus years and continue advising the most successful and helping winners win more.

Please do me a favor and help me continue to connect with winners in your sphere of influence, whether it's one on one, through social networks, on the web, or in your groups. Consider giving my books as gifts, sharing our websites, and personally connecting us to special successful people who thrive on going to the next level. We love encouraging people, changing their thinking, synergizing their teams, and impacting their success so they get more of the right RESULTS Faster!

VIPs from *Thinking: Change Your Thinking, Change Your Results*

(Note: You'll find VIPs—"Very Important Points" that highlight the takeaways and value points—in all my signature books. If you want to harvest the content or the value of the book quickly, the VIPs give you that delivery without your having to invest the time to read the entire book.)

1. Consistently achieving a high *Return on Effort* involves the pursuit of not only *great* results but *extraordinary* results.
2. When a business or a person achieves "greatness," they have difficulty grasping that there is yet a third possibility that awaits them: Mastery!
3. *It is a fact that the great motivational speakers of history have all based their teaching for producing individual change on helping people change what they think and believe about themselves and others.*

4. Thought is the most basic element in creating, planning, and executing any strategy.

5. Thinking is the root cause of success or failure.

6. The things you believe to be true are your mental constitution, and it is very difficult to think and accept ideas that conflict with what you believe to be true.

7. Strategic thinking can best be understood as thinking that focuses on execution of a vision, winning, and creating a competitive advantage.

DEDICATION

This book, the fifty books themselves, my life, and my legacy have all been profoundly impacted by a few very special people, or *People of Influence* (POIs), as I call them. I'm forever grateful that they poured their time, wisdom, insights, and experiences into my life, my business, and my work. Our lives can be supremely blessed by our relationships, and I cherish those I've been given

My Family

My grandparents, my parents, and my parents-in-law have all been a giant blessing to me. Here's an interesting fact: six couples in our family—my parents, Tammy's parents, and the two sets of grandparents on both sides—were blessed with over fifty years of marriage each, resulting in over three hundred years of marriage all together! That's more than three centuries of powerful marriage and relationship models poured into my life and into the life of our kids. It is my hope that this legacy of eternal and steadfast love continues in our family, generation after generation.

Mentors

Jinx Thompson, the father of my girlfriend Nancy Thompson when we were both sixteen, gave me *How to Win Friends and Influence People*, which opened my eyes to personal development and forever impacted my life.

Lanny Gardner and Lavell Rodgers took me under their wings in my twenties, and I will forever have fond memories of all the learning that took place during those special years. And about that same time, Richard Clipp demonstrated such amazing public speaking expertise and opened the door for me with Chrysler. That was life-changing for me.

Buz Barlow has been my attorney, colleague, protector, and very special friend for over thirty years. Buz is a man who loves people and loves helping me help others win. He's a model of professionalism from every angle.

Steve Dulin, Bill Arnold, and Lamar Smith have all had the greatest impact on our parenting success outside our family, helping Tammy and me see blind spots. They enabled us to better nourish two of the most extraordinary daughters a parent could ever wish for.

Jay Rodgers, my neighbor, co-author, and the most cherished entrepreneurial man I've ever met, has been pure gold as my business mentor. I sometimes think of Jay as my hitman, because he hits me over the head mentally and makes me see things I might have missed.

Peter Thomas is my mastermind partner, co-author, inspiration, example setter, business partner, world impacter, and cherished friend. Peter is a profound thinker who commissioned me to be his coach in his seventies and said, "Make me better."

Frank Halley has been an inspiration to me for two decades in the areas of business, fun, lifestyle, and smarts.

My great friend Brian Tracy has mentored me from afar and right up front. We've shared publishers, wisdom, connections, and cross-motivation. His mind and discipline are just plain rich!

The late Zig Ziglar was my mentor, co-author, inspirer, and example-setter.

Coaches

Mark Pantak, my coach for over thirty years now, studies even more than I do. I've said over the years I want to surround myself with the best (we all should), and Mark certainly fits the bill. He makes me think and enriches my life in such a selfless way, repeatedly.

Jim Norman went from being Zig Ziglar's president to being my coach and then my president. Jim shaped my thinking and impacted my life in colossal ways, as you have read about in this book. Jim and Zig, along with my dad, grandfather, and father-in-law—all fiercely devoted Christian men—have had the greatest positive impact on my life and my family legacy, and hence on the book you hold in your hands.

Special Friends and Team Members

Bill Connelly, my best friend for over thirty-five years

Nonie Jobe, my cherished, devoted, and time-giving writer, researcher, editor, and proofreader

Tawnya Austin, colleague, writer, and business overseer

Eloise Worden, my relationship manager, right-hand person, and my daily rock

My masterminds: Ross Lightle, Tony Martinez, Mark Magnacca, and the late, great Dr. Kevin Light

Jack Furst, my co-author, church-builder, and RESULTS! Center and business partner

Tammy Kling, my co-author and a megastar in my life who sharpens me and sharpens my books. She is a prolific writer and pushes me to think young and help my clients be inspired with her gift of words.

Clients

The many unique and cherished people we've been privileged to serve, who have trusted me to guide, coach, and advise them, their families, and their teams

Life Partner and My Foundation

Tammy Jeary, my wonderful, beautiful wife, extraordinary parenting partner, and life teammate

I thank all of you for allowing me to share life with you and learn from you.

TOP TONY JEARY COINED PHRASES

- **3-D Outline™:** A powerful outline format that includes the What, Why, and How aspects of a presentation and is used for shortening the meeting planning process (ask about TJI's 3-D Outline™ Builder Software)
- **Audience Champion:** A person in the audience who will openly support the presenter and reinforce his or her message
- **Breathing Space:** An opportunity to direct the attention of the audience away from the presenter in order to involve the audience more through a change of pace, and to give the presenter a moment to collect his or her thoughts (examples include showing a video, directing someone else to comment, or having audience members write something down—so their eyes come off the presenter for a few seconds or a few minutes)
- **Clarity, Focus, Execution:** The three core principles for Tony Jeary's *Strategic Acceleration* methodology

- **Critical Success Factor Template:** A summary of the key questions and answers required to achieve the highest performance in an important situation; can be an effective tool for a leader to manage accountability
- **Daily Performance Standards** (DPS): A concise list of operating procedures intended to provide clear direction relative to expected behavior and energy-spend by an organization's team members
- **Elegant Solution:** Being so clear on what you want to accomplish that three to five objectives can be simultaneously met through a single action
- **FPHESS:** Six areas of *Designing Your Own Life* goal-setting — Financial, Physical, Home life, Education, Social, and Spiritual
- **Help Us Help You** (HUHY): A form of Q&A in which audience members use 3 x 5 cards (electronically or physically) to communicate their questions/comments, so the presenter can then address the most common questions/comments during the Q&A session.
- **High Leverage Activities** (HLAs): The base methodology of Tony Jeary's bestselling book *Strategic Acceleration*; efficient actions that result in the most valuable outcomes
- **Life Team:** A group of hand-picked individuals who help you make decisions and execute (examples could include your spouse, executive assistant, coach, mentors, colleagues, readers, driver, lawyer, trainer, CPA, etc.)
- **MOLO** (More Of, Less Of): A simple exercise to help an individual or organization identify what they need to eliminate so they can focus on what matters most; an evaluation of what should be done more often and less often to ensure time is best invested on proactive, productive *HLAs* instead of on time-wasting, less effective tasks; allows top leaders to model self-reflection and continuous improvement
- **Operational Mastery:** Performing at the top level, better than great, often leading to extended value of an organization of any size

- **Planned Spontaneity:** Being so prepared you can respond to an audience in impromptu fashion; the better prepared you are the more spontaneity you can bring to your meetings and presentations with confidence
- **Presentation Arsenal:** A battery of weapons that consists of quotes, stories, statistics, printed and other visual material, wardrobe, electronic files we keep, and anything of substance that can help us make future presentations more colorful and effective
- **Presentation Universe:** All the presentation opportunities in a person's daily life, both personally and professionally
- **Production Before Perfection** (PBP): The principle that we must not allow the fear of potential missteps to prevent us from taking effective action now
- **Return on Effort** (ROE): Getting the best possible results from the most compressed amount of time and energy invested.
- **Strategic Acceleration:** Tony Jeary's proven methodology that helps people get clear, stay focused, and efficiently execute relevant, *High Leverage Activities*, thereby delivering results and success faster
- **Strategic Cascading:** The well-considered, consistent filtering down or across of messages throughout an organization or group (for example, from a top executive down to his/her direct reports down to their direct reports and so on; messages can also cascade across to other departments, and sometimes even upward in an organization)
- **Strategic Presence**: A leader's "personal brand," lived out through actions and words, that compels others to support objectives
- **Targeted Polling:** Calling on specific members of the audience and asking them to share their feedback, giving the presenter the ability to tailor the presentation to more successfully impact the audience; can be done before, during a break, or during an activity

- **Verbal Surveying:** Asking questions of the audience during a presentation to obtain usable feedback and then adjusting accordingly (i.e., speed up or slow down for more or less detail)

ABOUT THE AUTHOR

When many of the world's top achievers seek a strategic expert to help them accelerate their results, they are eventually drawn to Tony Jeary. Tony is the authority on RESULTS and has committed his career to studying and helping others think better and achieve more. If you want to better your life, your career, your organization, and your results, you need to know Tony.

Tony was raised by entrepreneurial parents and grandparents who thrived on identifying and pursuing new opportunities to serve others. His father taught him the powerful principle that has driven Tony's professional and personal life: "Always give more than is expected."

Exceeding expectations is the common thread that every Tony Jeary client experiences firsthand. Tony has advised people around the world (in some fifty countries) for over thirty years. He has published more than four dozen books, now in over a dozen languages. And he has worked with CEOs from many of the Fortune 500 companies and entrepreneurial families from the Forbes Richest 400.

Tony has been described as a "gifted encourager" who facilitates positive outcomes for others. His list of personal and professional relationships approaches 40,000 people, whom he connects with and nourishes out of his sincere interest and desire for shared success.

Tony's clients include individuals and organizations who are involved globally. He personally coaches the presidents of organizations like Ford, Walmart, Samsung, TGI Fridays, New York Life, Firestone, Sam's Club, and many more.

Tony has personal experience with both success and failure. He made and lost millions before he reached the age of thirty. That early experience with failure propelled him to help others live smart, live on purpose, and be their very best. Today he walks the talk and practices the distinctions that characterize success, both personally and professionally, sharing daily and encouraging others to think strategically about everything. He is blessed with a terrific marriage of over twenty-five years, two great daughters (both of whom he has co-authored books with), and one fantastic son-in-law.

Tony currently lives and works on his estate in the Dallas/Fort Worth area where his private RESULTS Studio is located.

info@tonyjeary.com

WHAT TONY JEARY INTERNATIONAL CAN DO FOR YOU

Results Coaching

Advice Matters, if it's the right advice. Having coached the world's top CEOs; published hundreds of books, videos, and courses; and advised clients in virtually every industry, across six continents, and at every stage of growth, Tony has positioned himself with a unique track record to take serious high achievers to a whole new level of results. He carefully selects a few clients to coach each year and is devoted to seeing those clients achieve extraordinary success.

Interactive Keynotes

Tony not only energizes, entertains, and educates; he also has his team work strategically and smartly with event teams to make his part as well as the entire experience a super win. An hour with Tony often changes people's lives forever and impacts an organization's results immediately. He delivers high value with a smart fun factor, and he freely shares best practices that both teams and people can really use.

Strategic Acceleration Facilitation Planning

Tony can do in a single day what takes many others days and even weeks to accomplish. He gets people to think strategically and has refined a process so powerful that the world travels to his RESULTS compound to experience clarity, focus, and the ability to synergistically execute. He provides at your fingertips three decades of best practices, processes, and tools for accelerating dramatic, sustained results in any organization.

Collaborative Relationships

TJI selectively partners with a handful of select organizations in an annual collaborative arrangement where we pour our knowledge and wisdom into the top leader(s) and their entire organization(s) and help build a super-charged, motivated, and engaged *High-Performing Team* We align with top entrepreneurs and C-Level management's vision and become an extension of them.

The bottom line is, we help: Clarify Vision and Focus on What Matters Most—*High Leverage Activities* (HLAs)—so people and entire organizations can execute and get the right results faster!

"Change your thinking change your results; it's that simple."

—Tony Jeary
Tonyjeary.com

Join us on the Results Faster! App

We are excited to share with you the Results Faster! app, which is available on the web for all devices. To get started, go to https:// tonyjeary.ihubapp.org and click the Login button in the top right corner. If this is your first time logging in, click on "Register."

Once registered, you then have instant access to our Gold Level channels, which include our most popular, most requested resources! Use the left-hand menu to view the channel numbers. Join any channels that are of interest to you, and the content will populate right on the home page of your Results Faster! app.